Critical Guides to Spanish Texts

70 García Márquez: Los funerales de la Mamá Grande

Critical Guides to Spanish Texts

EDITED BY ALAN DEYERMOND & STEPHEN HART

GARCÍA MÁRQUEZ

Los funerales de la Mamá Grande

Robin Fiddian

Professor of Spanish, University of Oxford
Fellow and Tutor in Spanish, Wadham College, Oxford

London
Grant & Cutler Ltd 2006

© Grant & Cutler Ltd 2006

ISBN-10: 07293 0446 9
ISBN-13: 978 07293 0446 7

Depósito legal: V. 3.383 - 2006

Printed in Spain by
Artes Gráficas Soler, S.L., Valencia
for
GRANT & CUTLER LTD
55–57 GREAT MARLBOROUGH STREET, LONDON W1F 7AY

Contents

For María and Elena — authors 'in their own write' — and Olaya, talented beyond words

Preface

Los funerales de la Mamá Grande by Gabriel García Márquez was first published in 1962 in Xalapa, Mexico, in a modest print run of two thousand copies. The next edition was by Editorial Sudamericana of Buenos Aires and coincided with the overnight success in 1967 of *Cien años de soledad* by the same author; a reprinting of the collection followed in 1969, and the rest, as they say, is history. At the University of Oxford and in Claremont, California, I have been fortunate enough to have access to library-held copies of the first edition of *Los funerales de la Mamá Grande*. Since the first edition is not universally available, I have restricted practical use of the two copies that I have consulted to record the page count of each of the eight stories that make up the collection. For the purposes of the present study, I have used Gabriel García Márquez, *Cuentos 1947–1992* (Barcelona, Buenos Aires and other locations including Santafé de Bogotá: Grupo Editorial Norma, 1996): as well as being widely available throughout the Hispanic world, this volume brings together all of the author's stories including those from the periods preceding and following the publication of *Los funerales de la Mamá Grande*. In Chapter One of this Critical Guide, I have occasion to refer to a number of stories from the earliest years of García Márquez's creative output (1947–1952). Subsequently collected and published under the title 'Ojos de perro azul' in 1972, their inclusion in the same volume as those of *Los funerales de la Mamá Grande* is a practical boon which allows me to dispense with separate editions and to limit all references to just one source, cited in parentheses in the text.

Parts of this study were tried out initially as conference papers and lectures at locations including the following: SOAS/University College London in October 2002; the University of Oregon at Portland in February–March 2003; University of Oxford in October

2003; Scripps College, Claremont, California, in March 2005; and Pepperdine University, Malibu, California, in November of that year. I am grateful to the organisers of all the events and forums at which I spoke for the opportunity to present my ideas about García Márquez to discerning audiences. I acknowledge the numerous contributions of groups and individuals everywhere and especially the responses of undergraduate and graduate students at Oxford, whose interest and encouragement have been important in bringing this Guide to completion.

1. Introduction

Los funerales de la Mamá Grande: Text/history/aesthetics

i. The history and pre-history of the text

Los funerales de la Mamá Grande (hereafter, *FMG*) comprises eight stories of varying length and subject that were published as a collection for the first time in Xalapa, Mexico in 1962. Prior to that, the stories had been produced piecemeal and without any planned or systematic interconnection other than the link to their author — relatively unknown outside his native Colombia until the publication of *Cien años de soledad* in 1967. There is an interesting anecdote concerning the loss, late in 1960, of the typescript of *FMG*, which García Márquez lent to a fellow Colombian writer, in prison in Mexico, who was avid for something to read. Álvaro Mutis took receipt of the typescript and then passed it on to the Mexican journalist Elena Poniatowska, who mislaid it. The typescript remained missing for some time but did eventually reappear, enabling publication by the Universidad Veracruzana in Xalapa, thanks in part to Mutis who had a contact there *(28*, p.73).

Apropos the history of the individual stories in *FMG*, the first and last had their imaginative roots in the early years of the previous decade, growing out of the same sub-soil that had given rise to *La hojarasca* (composed between 1950 and 1955) and 'Monólogo de Isabel viendo llover en Macondo' (first published under the title 'El invierno' in December 1952, and then under its definitive title in October–November 1955); this set of circumstances would lend credibility to the claim, made by several commentators of García Márquez's early work, that essentially he was engaged, throughout the period 1950–1955, in a single creative project which eventuated in a number of fragments marked by an unmistakable family resemblance. The majority of the stories in *FMG* had their origins in the later nineteen-fifties, and evinced a variety of styles and subject that differed appreciably from the output of the earlier years.

Research carried out, principally by Jacques Gilard, into the chronology of the stories that make up *FMG* allows us to account with some exactitude for the order of their composition and probable completion. First in the sequence was 'Un día después del sábado', completed in 1954 (*5, IV*, p.55, n.53) and awarded a national literary prize in the following year. Next came 'Un día de éstos', 'La siesta del martes' and 'En este pueblo no hay ladrones', on which García Márquez is known to have worked in the first half of 1958, finishing the first mentioned of the triptych as early as March of that year. The second half of 1958 saw García Márquez bring to completion three more stories: 'La prodigiosa tarde de Baltazar', 'La viuda de Montiel' and 'Rosas artificiales' (*5, IV*, pp.71–73). Last but not least, since it would come to supply the title for the volume, 'Los funerales de la Mamá Grande' dates from the middle of 1959 — a year which represents a watershed in Caribbean and Latin American political history and whose significance needs to be borne in mind when eventually assessing the wide range of intention and meaning in 'Los funerales de la Mamá Grande'.

The clarity of outline in the sequence plotted above justifies the adoption of a chronological approach to the stories in the volume, viewed as a number of discrete moments in a linear process. In the main sections of this Guide, the order of composition of the stories will be a prominent consideration, given the existence, plain to see, of a frame constituted by the first and last stories and encompassing the period 1954 to 1959 inclusive. It is nevertheless important to acknowledge that, in the period concerned, García Márquez worked on other texts in addition to the stories of *FMG*, thus making it advisable to adopt a certain breadth and flexibility of approach to an output which also comprised *El coronel no tiene quien le escriba* (published in 1957) and *La mala hora* (1962), both of which reflect narrative and thematic details of the stories under consideration here. The best approach to the stories in *FMG* is therefore one that is many-layered: attentive throughout to relations amongst the stories themselves and to connections with other contemporary works by García Márquez, but equally sensitive to the peculiarities of individual stories, viewed as bounded and unique.

It is useful, at this point, to attempt to situate the stories of *FMG* within the general sweep of García Márquez's work and to view them, particularly, in relation to the dozen or so short narratives written by the author over the period 1947 to 1952. A brief excursion into the realm of what Mario Vargas Llosa symptomatically called the 'pre-history' of García Márquez's literary career (*28*, p.217) will shed light on the generic and aesthetic background against which his later work evolved and acquired the outlines and characteristics for which it is universally known today.

In Vol. I of his exquisitely crafted memoirs, García Márquez confirms that his first four stories were 'La tercera resignación' (1947), 'Eva está dentro de su gato' (1947), 'Tubal Caín forja una estrella' (1948), and 'La otra costilla de la muerte' (1948) (*1*, pp. 297, 300 & 393); these were followed by 'Diálogo del espejo' (1949), 'Amargura para tres sonámbulos' (1949), 'Ojos de perro azul' (1950), 'La mujer que llegaba a las seis' (1950), 'La noche de los alcaravanes' (1950), 'Alguien desordena estas rosas' (1950), and 'Nabo, el negro que hizo esperar a los ángeles' (1951) (*5*, I, pp.57–70); finally, there appeared 'El invierno' (1952), published — as we have already seen — under the revised title of 'Monólogo de Isabel viendo llover en Macondo', in 1955 (*5*, IV, pp.77–78).

In his authoritative 1971 overview of the fiction of García Márquez up to and including *Cien años de soledad*, Mario Vargas Llosa detected in the first five stories a common thematic source, narrative style and aesthetic which he ascribed to the author's late 1940s fascination with Franz Kafka (*28*, p.218). Scenarios of nightmare and sickness, accidents and death constitute the narrative matrix of these early stories, exemplified in 'La tercera resignación'. Here, a consciousness experiences, with an almost unbearable acuteness of sensation, the delirium and horror of the

living dead. Identified with a young man who died for the first time
aged seven and who has been laid out in a coffin for the past
eighteen years, the consciousness anticipates a second death and
burial brought on by the irremediable decomposition of his body,
and eventually succumbs to the prospect of a third and final death,
accepted out of lethargy and resignation. At the level of narrative
technique, García Márquez employs a third person interior
focalization reminiscent of Kafka's *Metamorphosis* — a work that
he later acknowledged as the inspiration behind 'La tercera
resignación' (*1*, p.296). Constructed around a sequence of verbs
referring to mental rather than physical activity, the internal drama
of the story is rendered immediate to the reader by the insistent use
of the temporal marker 'ahora'. In the latter part of the story, a shift
from the preterite to the conditional and future tenses opens the
narrative perspective out onto a moment that lies beyond the
temporal frame of the story and onto a space that is located
underground, in a cemetery; the penultimate paragraph also exploits
an association between physical dissolution, sweat and uterine fluid,
that suggests a partly conscious desire to return to the womb (p.23).

The link between psychological themes and fantastic
situations of the kind described here has been documented in an
important essay by the Chilean critic, S. Meckled, on themes of the
uncanny in García Márquez's work. Drawing on Sigmund Freud
and Otto Rank, Meckled highlights the presence, in García
Márquez's early stories, of motifs including 'mirrors and the
"double", castration dreams and terrors, uncanny fantasies of death
and of life after death, fantasies and fears of intrauterine life [...],
dream-scapes and fantasies centred on symbols of castration
(blindness or self-blinding as in *Oedipus Rex*; razors, scissors and
knives, all stock symbols of castration [...])' (*47*, p.110). Several of
the themes and motifs listed by Meckled come together in 'La otra
costilla de la muerte', which can legitimately be read as an
exploration of psychic neurosis and obsession. Beyond the handful
of stories analysed by Meckled, the themes of sight and blindness
also appear in 'Amargura para tres sonámbulos', 'Diálogo del
espejo', 'Ojos de perro azul' , and 'La noche de los alcaravanes',

and the motif of invisibility in 'Alguien desordena estas rosas'. This thematic repetition points to a definite susceptibility on the author's part to concerns about sight and loss of sight, and to an intensification and re-ordering of the senses in the narratives, where hearing, touch and smell are often emphasized at the expense of sight. Tied in with a questioning of conventional models of time and space, this undermining of the claims of sight — encapsulated in the empiricist dictum, 'Seeing is believing' — is wholly consistent with the anti-Realist, fantastic orientation of García Márquez's writing at this stage of his career.

The assertion of coherence made by Vargas Llosa is certainly borne out in the above comments on the five stories that were written by García Márquez between 1947 and 1949. It does not, however, apply in the same way to the stories written between 1950 and 1952, where the (broadly) Kafkaesque model of writing is displaced in some instances by a new one, identified, principally, with William Faulkner and Virginia Woolf. As early as April 1950, García Márquez lamented the generalized stagnation of Colombian prose narrative and called on his fellow writers to open themselves up to foreign influences:

Todavía no se ha escrito en Colombia la novela que esté indudable y afortunadamente influida por los Joyce, por Faulkner o por Virginia Woolf. Y he dicho 'afortunadamente' porque no creo que podríamos los colombianos ser, por el momento, una excepción al juego de las influencias. En su prólogo a 'Orlando', Virginia [sic] confiesa sus influencias. Faulkner mismo no podría negar la que ha ejercido sobre él, el mismo Joyce. Algo hay — sobre todo en el manejo del tiempo — entre Huxley y otra vez Virginia Woolf. Franz Kafka y Proust andan sueltos por la literatura del mundo moderno. Si los colombianos hemos de decidirnos acertadamente, tendríamos que caer irremediablemente en esta corriente. Lo lamentable es que ello no haya acontecido

aún, ni se vean los más ligeros síntomas de que pueda
acontecer alguna vez. (*5*, I, p.269)

This call to modernization combines a palpable sense of urgency
with an absolute conviction that the absorption of foreign cultural
models stands to benefit Colombian writing as it has benefited
modern writers the world over. At the level of detail, what is most
noteworthy are the names that are cited as examples of the welcome
traffic of influences in contemporary world fiction: Joyce, Faulkner,
Woolf, Huxley, Proust, and Kafka represent the highest achievements of European and North American modernist fiction and are
held up as the supreme agents of a process of transculturation and
literary renewal that is assumed to be vital to the well-being of
Colombian writing at and beyond the mid point of the twentieth
century.

The story of García Márquez's own encounters with work by
these authors is told in outline in the pages of his autobiography,
Vivir para contarla. After an early (and failed) attempt to get to
grips with Joyce's *Ulysses* (*1*, p.295) and an engagement with Kafka
that produced mixed results (according to García Márquez, reading
Metamorphosis in 1947 was an overpowering experience for him [*1*,
p.300]), he read a translation of *Mrs Dalloway* by Virginia Woolf,
along with earlier works by Herman Melville (*Moby Dick*) and
Nathaniel Hawthorne (*The House of the Seven Gables*), which left a
lasting impression on him (*1*, pp.406–07). Then, towards the end of
1949, he acquired translations of at least four books by Faulkner and
a second by Woolf (*Orlando*), which he later credited with releasing
him from a 'creative limbo' (*1*, p.422) and enabling him to write in
a vein that was no longer tentative and second-hand but, rather,
authentic and self-assured.

Commentators have amassed a wealth of evidence of the
influence of Faulkner, especially *The Sound and the Fury* and *As I
Lay Dying*, on García Márquez's first novel, *La hojarasca* (see *48* &
51).The substance of their claims is confirmed by the author himself
in Chapter 7 of *Vivir para contarla*, where he acknowledges taking
the narrative situation of *As I Lay Dying* and using it to frame a

community-drama set in a fictional Colombian backwater to which he gave the name 'Macondo'. He further explains, 'Los autores que me estimularon más para escribir [*La hojarasca*] fueron los novelistas norteamericanos [...] sobre todo por las afinidades de toda índole que encontraba entre las culturas del sur profundo y la del Caribe, con la que tengo una identificación absoluta, esencial e insustituible en mi formación de ser humano y escritor' (*1*, p.440).

Faulkner's depiction of the Deep South in terms of stagnation born of defeat; families, incest and hereditary evil; the conflict between Puritanism and depravity; ethnic stratification; and the heroic compulsion to persevere and resist, is implicit in this reference to a cultural heritage with which García Márquez would have found it easy to identify, notwithstanding fundamental differences of language, religion and economic development between Caribbean Spanish America and the southern states of the USA.

The stated chronology of García Márquez's encounters with works by Faulkner, Woolf and others ties in not only with the writing of *La hojarasca* but also with that of stories including 'Nabo, el negro que hizo esperar a los ángeles' (1951) and 'El invierno' (1952), both of which betray the influence of Faulkner; another item in the Faulknerian vein is 'Un día después del sábado' (1954), which García Márquez would eventually include in *FMG* (1962). 'Nabo, el negro que hizo esperar a los ángeles' tells the story of a black boy who was hired to look after a retarded child and suffered a kick in the head from a horse, which reduced him to a state of idiocy; some fifteen years later, he breaks free from his physical enclosure in an explosion of 'feroz animalidad' (p.94). Especially disturbing for the reader is the sub-text of Nabo's abuse at the hands of the owners of the estate: it is relayed through a first-person-plural narrative voice which alternates with a third-person omniscient voice and disavows any responsibility for the inhumane treatment of Nabo ever since his accident. Structurally, the story exploits repetition and flashback as vehicles for rendering the closed and obsessive world of Nabo's consciousness. With the example of Benjy, in *The Sound and the Fury*, and the social milieu of countless other Faulknerian narratives in mind, Mario Vargas Llosa had no hesitation in labeling 'Nabo, el negro que hizo esperar a los ángeles' 'el más faulkneriano de los relatos [of the early 1950s]' (*28*, p.228). For Mary A. Kilmer-Tchalekian, the story demonstrates Márquez's growing mastery of his art, illustrated in the successful assimilation of the example of Faulkner (*45*, p.35).

'El invierno' stands in an equally close relationship to Faulkner. Filleted out of *La hojarasca* for separate publication in 1952, the story attests to five days of rain that falls on a provincial town, and is seen from the perspective of a young married woman, Isabel. Catholic, pregnant and susceptible to sense-disturbance, she reacts to the metereological 'catastrophe' (p.112) by becoming confused about time and the people around her and reaches a point at the end of the story where she is no longer certain whether she is alive or dead (At least one critic asserts that she is narrating from the afterlife, [*30*, p.25]). Isabel's mental vagueness is offset by a strong sense of household and the community to which she belongs. Hers, or rather her stepmother's, is a household of criollos tended by servants from an exploited ethnic group ('guajiros'); the household is visited every Tuesday by a beggar woman who relies on neighbourhood charity; and there is a local institution for blind girls who receive payment for singing 'cancioncillas' on their weekly visits to the house. In spite of their abstract, metaphysical character, Isabel's perceptions serve as a valuable filter for the projection of a finely-drawn picture of social and economic relations in the community that is Macondo.

Isabel's monologue — to refer to the story by its later, definitive title — interrelates in significant ways with two other stories in *Ojos de perro azul*, which are 'Eva está dentro de su gato' of 1947 and 'La mujer que llegaba a las seis' of 1950. The first of these shares with 'El invierno'/ 'Monólogo de Isabel viendo llover en Macondo' a concern regarding the oppression of women under patriarchy, explored through the medium of a female consciousness that is semi-resistant in the case of Eva and utterly colonized in the case of Isabel. It is perhaps surprising, given its title, that 'Eva está dentro de su gato' has failed to elicit any critical response in terms of its gender implications; yet the story, touched on by Fernando

Burgos in a survey-type study (*33*, pp.465–67), is an acute examination of the burden on women of gender stereotypes and an important forerunner of later works by García Márquez that will be centered around women.

'La mujer que llegaba a las seis' also gives pride of place in its plot to a female character, thus linking with 'Monólogo de Isabel viendo llover en Macondo'. The two stories are, however, different in key respects: first, the two main characters are polar opposites in terms of life-style and circumstances, the woman in the earlier story being a prostitute who has almost certainly committed a murder; and second, in respect of narrative style, 'La mujer que llegaba a las seis' follows the model, not of Faulkner, but of Hemingway, whose economical and objective prose-style represents a 'third way' — an alternative to Kafka and Faulkner — in the author's narrative development in the early fifties. As noted by Ángel Rama (*53*, pp. 9–13), Márquez's writing at this point displays an openness to contrary styles: having largely outgrown the model of Kafka, he remains committed to Faulkner but is drawn also to the models of Hemingway and others, including Graham Greene. The eclecticism demonstrated in this attitude will be reflected in the eight stories written between 1954 and 1959 that will make up *FMG*. There, the Faulknerian model is retained initially but soon eclipsed by Hemingway, until both Faulkner and Hemingway are in turn displaced by yet another model, which derives from the oral style of folk narrative and offers a versatile vehicle for representing and critiquing the real.

ii. Los funerales de la Mamá Grande: Aesthetics and culture

The preceding account of the major narrative precursors of *FMG* prepares the ground for some more detailed consideration of García Márquez's aesthetic creed and broader cultural outlook over the period during which he wrote the stories in the collection. Naturally, where that creed and outlook crystallize in the purest form is in the stories themselves, but they can also be inferred from other sources broadly contemporary with the writing of the stories. The most useful point of reference in this regard is the series of journalistic essays penned by García Márquez between 1948 and 1960, when he worked for a number of newspapers, first, on the Colombian *costa*, and then in Bogotá; thereafter, as correspondent in a number of European capitals, in both Western Europe and the Eastern block; and finally, in Venezuela and other locations in the Americas, to which he returned in 1958. A set of comments on a variety of topics, primarily in the fields of literature and cinema, sketch out the rudiments of an aesthetic and cultural creed that can be taken as valid for the period and collection under review.

In several dozen articles written from 1948 on, García Márquez discussed work by authors ranging from Edgar Allan Poe, William Faulkner and Aldous Huxley, to Colombian writers living on the northern *costa* who were his contemporaries, such as Rafael Marriaga, José Félix Fuenmayor and Álvaro Cepeda Salmudio. Between February 1954 and June 1955 he also reviewed one hundred and eighty films from countries including the USA, Italy, Spain, and Argentina, showing a particular fondness for canonical works by the Italian neorealist directors, Roberto Rossellini, Vittorio de Sica and Cesare Zavattini.

In his analyses of cinematic narratives of that time, García Márquez placed a high premium on realism, involving, amongst other things, a faithful depiction of historical environment and the social conditions obtaining therein. A review of 'La ronda del sospechoso' (originally, *Stranger on the Prowl*, dir. Joseph Losey, 1952), praises the 'fidelidad' of the film's representation of life in post-war Rome, and compares it favourably with examples of earlier cinema: 'La pintura de la vida social de postguerra ha sido lograda con tanta fidelidad como en los buenos films neorrealistas' (*5*, II, p.267). Similar praise is accorded to the Spanish landmark film, *Bienvenido, Mr Marshall* (1952), for the unprecedented way in which it mirrors the experience of the Spanish people: 'Por primera vez un grupo de jóvenes cineastas ha puesto frente al mundo al verdadero pueblo español tan minuciosa y auténticamente conocido a través de la literatura.' Commenting on the performance of Pepe Isbert in the role of the town's mayor, García Márquez observes, 'Este alcalde [...] es un alcalde de carne y hueso que vive en la pantalla con la fuerza de la realidad', adding, 'Y así todos los personajes: el cura, el embaucador, la bailarina y el hidalgo, que en virtud de un tratamiento concienzudo y entrañable, dejaron de ser pintorescas postales para turistas y se convirtieron en seres vivientes' (*5*, II, p.124). Realism, in this context, is synonymous with verisimilitude and 'lifelikeness' and takes for granted the capability of narrative art to provide accurate representations of 'life' and 'reality'.

Mirácolo a Milano (1950) by De Sica seems to move outside the conventional frame of realism being traced here: drawing on stock motifs of fairy tale and fantastic literature, it mixes 'lo real y lo fantástico, hasta el extremo de que en muchos casos no es posible saber dónde termina lo uno y dónde comienza lo otro' (*5*, II, p.174). Yet it, too, emits a 'carga de verdad' and 'palpitación de vida' which make it, in the final analysis, 'una película extraordinaria [,] convincente, humana, iluminada constantemente por el soplo de la genialidad' (*5*, II, p.175). The notions of a charge and 'palpitación de vida' are all-important, since they bring us close to the neo-realist aesthetic of Rossellini and its explication by Rossellini's great admirer, André Bazin (*58*, pp.23–40). The notions also identify a moral dimension that ranks high in García Márquez's scale of values: for, in addition to praising the mimesis of narrative art, he expects that such works should delve into and illuminate the human condition. Perhaps the most compelling representation of historically-inflected human drama is *Ladri di biciclette* (1948) by De Sica, described as 'la película más humana que jamás se haya realizado' (*5*, I, p.467).

Art and ethics coincide for García Márquez at another level, which is that of cultural politics. Along with a commitment to verisimilitude and fundamental human values, the Colombian writer also defends the cultural integrity of his native Latin America. More than a quarter of a century before he delivered his famous Nobel Prize address asking for acknowledgment of the particularity of Latin American culture vis-à-vis that of the developed world (*6*, pp.207–11), García Márquez insists on the worth of local and continental cultural production, with certain, significant qualifications. Already in 1950, commenting on 'Un viejo cuento de escopetas' by his fellow Colombian, José Félix Fuenmayor, Márquez upholds the story's claims to universality and affirms its equal standing vis-à-vis the very best of writing in the short-story form at the time, as represented by 'la cuentística norteamericana'. In García Márquez's assessment, Fuenmayor has exploited to the full the examples of Faulkner, Hemingway, Steinbeck, et al, and produced a narrative of technical mastery comparable to theirs. This is not to say that his writing is derivative. Essentially, Fuenmayor has adapted 'los mejores recursos' of North American writing to the local subject matter of life in Colombia and achieved a 'legítimo costumbrismo' of the nation. As important as technical know-how is the 'ángulo humano' from which Fuenmayor approaches his material: 'escribe como los norteamericanos, porque se coloca en el mismo ángulo humano y sabe decir las cosas de aquí, con tan buenos recursos, con tanta precisión, con tanto dramatismo, como los norteamericanos dicen las de su Norteamérica' (*5*, I, p.325). Taking aspects of Colombian society as his subject, Fuenmayor succeeds in extracting from them their essential, universal significance: 'Se va al fondo, a la esencia de lo nuestro, y saca a flote nuestras características nacionales. Pero solamente las que tienen valor universal' (*5*, I, p.326).The local and the universal thus fuse in Fuenmayor's story, which can compete on equal terms with the very best fiction coming out of the United States.

It is significant that García Márquez privileges the cultural products of the Colombian *costa* over those of the capital of the nation, Bogotá. In a swingeing rebuke dated 1950, the author remarks on the 'exclusivismo parroquial de los portaestandartes capitalinos' and observes, 'El provincianismo literario en Colombia empieza a dos mil quinientos metros sobre el nivel del mar' (*5*, I, p.273). A decade later, he renews the accusation, charging that 'La literatura colombiana [...] ha sido un fraude a la nación' (*5*, IV, p.793). *Costa* culture remains exempt from his criticism. Indeed, there is a very real sense in which he promotes it as both superior to what is produced in the capital and as possessing an inherent worth and vigour that measure up to the value of cultural products anywhere, whether they be films shot in Rome or Berlin or stories written in locations in the USA.

This cult of the local manifests itself in numerous essays devoted not only to the educated literary culture of cities like Barranquilla, but also to the popular music and lore of the region of Valledupar and other rural locations in Colombia. A set of four essays written in 1952 for serial publication in a magazine entitled *Lámpara* celebrate the peculiarities of a northern inland region known as 'La Sierpe', in a localist idiom which combines humour and fantasy with the objective manner of reportage. Collected under the title 'Un país en la Costa Atlántica', the essays draw on legends with which García Márquez and others were familiar and which, according to his biographer, he attempted to verify in trips to the reputed location of La Sierpe towards the end of the 1940s (*2*, p. 260). As related in his memoirs, the author on one occasion had a train of mules loaded with provisions and was all set to leave in search of this 'país de leyenda', but circumstances intervened and forced a postponement of the adventure (*1*, p.419)!

The essays about La Sierpe describe a swampy region with an infernal climate and sparse population. In a transparent mimicry of the discourses of anthropology and documentary, the author, who is also the narrator of the essays, accounts for the religious and social practices of the region's inhabitants, who, he attests, 'son católicos convencidos, pero practican la religión a su manera, como la mayoría de los campesinos colombianos' (*5*, II, p.118). What distinguishes the inhabitants from other Colombians is their belief in 'la Marquesita de la Sierpe'. Older generations used to recall stories about 'una española bondadosa y menuda, dueña de una fabulosa riqueza' who lived alone in 'una casa grande y suntuosa en el centro de la que ahora es conocida como La Ciénaga de la Sierpe'; endowed with a range of supernatural powers, she commanded widespread respect and 'era una especie de gran mamá de quienes le servían'. In the present (i.e. in 1952 and after), the 'Marquesita' continues to be the object of a religious cult and lives on in numerous legends that tell of her fabulous riches and far-reaching powers (*5*, II, p.119).

In Chapter 7 of his memoirs, García Márquez provides an invaluable gloss on the aesthetics of the essays about 'La Sierpe'. He recalls how a group of friends and advisors in Barranquilla 'estaban de acuerdo en que la fórmula del reportaje había sido la más adecuada para un tema que estaba en la peligrosa frontera de lo que no podía creerse'; he also adds the telling rider that 'Alvaro Mutis se mostraba seguro de que esa clase de reportajes podían ser un puntillazo al costumbrismo chato en sus propios terrenos' (*1*, pp.506–07). The statements emphasize the interdependence between the subject matter of the essays and the author's choice of an appropriate style of writing: at the same time as he acknowledges the popular provenance of the material about La Sierpe, García Márquez does not shy away from claiming a crucial role in its narrative elaboration. Importantly, the first of the statements gives prominence to the issue of credibility, whilst the second makes a retrospective claim that the essays were motivated by a determination to beat *costumbrismo* at its own game: it would do this by aping the characteristics of a regionalist writing that had traditionally been interested primarily in local types and customs, but it would break with the aesthetic tenets of a conventional documentary realism.

Looked at from the vantage point of the twenty-first century, García Márquez's project was path-breaking and seminal. The essays about La Sierpe represent an artistic achievement that includes, in particular, the creation of a narrative tone that will become one of the hallmarks of later writing by the author, especially the stories of *La increíble y triste historia de la cándida Eréndira y su abuela desalmada* and *El otoño del patriarca*. In terms of narrative mode, the essays act as a blueprint for a new, expanded kind of realism, one which accommodates local myths and legends and other aspects of a people's collective mindset, adapted for the purposes of analysis and critique. Finally, at the level of cultural politics, the essays about La Sierpe promote local values over and above those that are conceived as universal: this is most visible in the narrative depiction of 'la Marquesita de la Sierpe', who comes across as both a local variant and a parody of the archetypal 'Great Mother' reconstructed from a huge range of sources by Erich Neumann in a weighty tome published, coincidentally, in 1955 (see *75*). Diverging from the ahistoric abstraction and universal pretensions of archetype, la Mamá Grande originates in a local Spanish American context that is rooted in historical circumstance and inflected with superstition and ignorance that the author exposes wittily and exploits to playful effect.

iii. The short story in Spanish America and critical strategies for reading it

The *cuento* is a jewel in the crown of modern Spanish American literature, with antecedents that can be traced back to the Colonial period and, in the opinion of some of its commentators, to pre-Colombian times in America as well. The form enjoyed some success in the nineteenth century and then flourished early in the twentieth in the hands of writers such as Horacio Quiroga (Uruguay 1878–1937), working under the spell of Edgar Allan Poe and Nathaniel Hawthorne, and Leopoldo Lugones (Argentina 1874–1938). The publication, in 1944, of *Ficciones* by Jorge Luis Borges (Argentina 1899–1986) was a landmark event in the history of short fiction in Spanish America: within a decade, Borges's works would inspire a legion of writers including Juan Rulfo and Carlos Fuentes, both of Mexico, and Julio Cortázar of Argentina, by then living in Europe. The very first stories of García Márquez can be considered part of this wider phenomenon, along with those of the mid- to late nineteen fifties which are the primary object of study in this Guide.

In respect of García Márquez's domestic affiliations, a contemporary tradition of Colombian short story writing is attested to in Eduardo Pachón Padilla's anthology and other collections, where authors represented include Francisco Gómez Escobar, Adel López Gómez and Alfonso Bonilla Naar (see *77*). Interestingly, García Márquez disparaged the achievements of the short story within the Colombian literary tradition. In his view, poetry held the highest rank in the national pantheon, followed a good distance behind by the novel with a mere handful of titles that 'sobrevivieron a su tiempo'; languishing at the foot of the order of merit was the short story, which had failed to prosper for the simple reason that it 'había naufragado en una retórica escarpada y sin alma' (*1*, pp.306–07). Leaving the substance of the author's assessment to one side, the perception of the absence of a thriving tradition of short story writing in Colombia goes some way to explaining García Márquez's insistence, around the late nineteen-forties, on the advantages to be gained from the fertilisation of Colombian fiction by outside, foreign influences.

A factor that inhibited the growth of the short story in Spanish America in the nineteenth century was the absence of a home-grown tradition of critical thinking about the form. Spanish American letters of the Romantic and post-Romantic periods spawned no document equivalent to Poe's 'Philosophy of Composition' or the same author's reviews of fictional works by Nathaniel Hawthorne, for example. That deficiency would eventually be remedied up to a point by Horacio Quiroga early in the twentieth century, in essays including 'El manual del perfecto cuentista' and 'Decálogo para el perfecto cuentista' (see *79*). I say 'up to a point' because Quiroga's Ten Commandments are far from uniformly serious and cannot be construed as a systematic poetics of the *cuento*. Overall, however, the Uruguayan author's essays demonstrate a level of professionalism and an awareness of the artistic possibilities of the form that outstrip by far any earlier attempt to theorise the short story in Spanish America. In the wider scheme of Spanish American literary history, Quiroga's essays are important fundamentally as forerunners of more sophisticated work by later writers such as Borges, Cortázar and Rosario Ferré. 'El arte narrativo y la magia' (1932) by the first of this trio expounds certain principles of form and aesthetics that will feature in the analysis of one of the stories of *FMG*, below.

We have already registered García Márquez's youthful enthusiasm for writers such as Poe, Hawthorne, Kafka, Faulkner and Hemingway. The case of Hemingway merits special attention on account of the canonical status of many of his stories, the acuteness of his theoretical insights into the short story form, and García Márquez's stated familiarity with, and acknowledged debt to a range of his work. As noted by Aden W. Hayes and others, García Márquez had read a large number of stories by Hemingway, as early as 1952 (*42*, p.53). In a series of articles that he wrote that year and in 1953, he expressed his admiration for the American author's achievements in 'Cat in the Rain', 'The Killers', 'Ten Indians', and 'Today is Friday', reserving his highest praise for 'The Short Happy Life of Francis Macomber', which he would subsequently describe somewhat colloquially as 'el mejor cuento que se haya escrito. Un cuento cojonudo'(*73*, p.149). Soon after writing 'La mujer que llegaba a las seis', García Márquez admitted sheepishly, in a letter to a friend dated March 1952, that 'el cuento parece más de Hemingway que de G.G.M. [sic]' (*5*, I, p.725).

An important part of Hemingway's legacy to García Márquez and others was the theoretical pronouncements he made about the short story, in particular his conception of the iceberg principle, which he explained in *Death in the Afternoon* and elsewhere:

> If a writer of prose knows enough about what he is writing about he may omit things that he knows and the reader, if the writer is writing truly enough, will have a feeling of those things as strongly as though the writer had stated them. The dignity of movement of an iceberg is due to only one-eighth of it being above water. (*68*, p.77)

This and other similar statements resonated powerfully with García Márquez, who cited it on several occasions — in October 1959, for example (*5*, IV, p.766). Concomitantly, Hemingway's advocacy of economy and restraint ('Eschew the monumental. Shun the Epic' [*68*, p.79]); his ideal of the 'true simple declarative sentence' (*68*, p.28); his pursuit of authenticity ('You see I'm trying in all my stories to get the feeling of the actual life process across — not just depict life — or criticize it — but to actually make it alive. So that when you have read something by me you actually experience the thing' [*68*, p.33]); and so apparently trivial a detail as his mistrust of adjectives and similes (*68*, p.38), are all specifically relevant to

García Márquez's creative project and to a sympathetic understanding of it. In practical terms and as a single example of a lesson
learnt from a master craftsman, we might consider a detail of the
narrative technique of 'The Short Happy Life of Francis
Macomber', where Hemingway suddenly switches the narrative
perspective from Macomber the hunter to a lion that he has
wounded, and back to Macomber. This device finds its way very
promptly into the work of García Márquez, where a similar shift of
perspective occurs in the first story of *FMG*, dramatising the
relationship between two different characters in 'Un día después del
sábado' (see below).

Another major point of reference in an informed survey of
García Márquez's relation to the tradition of the short story is the
Russian pre-modernist, Anton Chekhov (1860–1904). To my
knowledge, the Colombian author has made no explicit mention of
Chekhov in any of his public declarations, and only a handful of
critics (see *20* and *40*) have suggested any connection between the
two writers. Yet, the crucial importance of Chekhov in the development of the modern short story, of which he is widely regarded as
the father, ties him inevitably to García Márquez, who would have
received his influence indirectly at least, filtered through the work
and example of James Joyce, Virginia Woolf and Hemingway.

A devotee of Chekhov, Virginia Woolf recognized in the
Russian author's work specific elements of form and content that
marked him out as a precursor of Modernism, including the
attenuation of plot, narrative rhythm and a visionary metaphysics.
Writing in 1919, she acknowledged the Chekhovian innovation of
inconclusiveness and stated 'We are by this time alive to the fact
that inconclusive stories are legitimate' (*81*, p.85) — an observation
that holds good for García Márquez's handling of narrative, four
decades later, in 'La siesta del martes'. The 'sentimental
counterpoint' detected by Renato Poggioli (*78*, pp.109–30) in a
range of stories by Chekhov is a feature of the Russian author's
work that permeates that of Hemingway and finds its way also into
stories by García Márquez. The interplay of pathos and irony that
informs 'A Gentleman Friend', for example, and the undercurrents

of emotion that circulate in other stories, anticipate the tonality and spectrum of feeling evoked in 'En este pueblo no hay ladrones' and 'Rosas artificiales', where the narrative sympathy rests largely with the women characters, as it does in countless stories by Chekhov. Narrative attitude and sensibility constitute a central point of comparability between Gabriel García Márquez and Anton Chekhov — 'a writer endowed with keen psychological and ethical insight', in the words of Poggioli (*78,* p.116), and one whose 'compassion was all-encompassing, but never sentimental', in those of Rosamund Bartlett (*60,* p.xi).

The poetic construction of the modern short story arguably has its primary origin in the work of Chekhov and provides one of the practical, methodological underpinnings of the present Critical Guide. In the chapters that follow, I look at the stories of *FMG* with the closeness of attention usually reserved for poems. To be sure, the eight stories in the collection are superb examples of narrative artistry in areas including plot, structure, point of view, character, dialogue, and setting, and I give those aspects due weight in the pages that follow. However, poetic features including imagery, motif and allusion are equally important in the creation of aesthetic effects, and I seek to account for them too in my appreciation of the stories' designs.

It is appropriate at this point to make a brief comment about the organisation of this Guide. With one exception, I take the stories, not in the order of their appearance in the first and all subsequent editions of *FMG,* but in the order of their composition. This chronological approach breaks, most notably, with the author's own preferred order, which placed 'La siesta del martes' at the head of the volume. However, a chronological approach allows for the gradual emergence of a set of patterns relating, inter alia, to mode, character, style, and thematic concerns, which become apparent as the sequence of eight stories unfolds. The first two chapters that follow are devoted, inter alia, to introducing the two major settings of the collection. Subsequent chapters build on that sense of time and place and other aspects of the depicted fictional worlds. The thematic focus sharpens with a concentration on issues of gender in

Chapters Four and Five. Chapter Six addresses a range of literary and political aspects of the title-story which represent an apparent departure from norms established earlier in the collection; with the benefit of hindsight, it is possible to distinguish continuities as well as discontinuities between 'Los funerales de la Mamá Grande' and its precursors, and this is acknowledged in a Conclusion which recapitulates salient features of the stories and provides a synthetic overview of the volume.

2. A sense of time and place: two stories of Macondo

'Un día después del sábado'

i. Introduction

In the standard editions of *FMG*, 'Un día después del sábado' appears in sixth place, sandwiched between 'La viuda de Montiel' and 'Rosas artificiales', both written in the second half of 1958. However, the story was in fact the earliest written and dates from 1954. The award of a prize by Colombia's Association of Artists and Writers the following year coincided with the publication of García Márquez's inaugural novel, *La hojarasca*, and has been seen by Raymond Williams in retrospect as representing a breakthrough in the author's literary career (30, p.10). 'Un día después del sábado' and *La hojarasca* also belong together in a substantial sense, comprising, with 'Monólogo de Isabel viendo llover en Macondo', a tightly-knit trio of texts fictionalising Macondo and written under the common influence of William Faulkner. 'Un día después del sábado' draws on the same provincial ambience and location as 'Monólogo de Isabel...' and *La hojarasca*; the historical and social parameters of the narrative are identical to the ones delineated in those texts; and 'Un día después del sábado' explores further the personal and collective consciousness of Macondo, taking a different but complementary set of individuals as the object of its analysis.

ii. The narrative

The narrative of 'Un día después del sábado' is parsimonious with geographical details, but the mention of Manaure, some hours away by train, and the presence of the Hotel Macondo are sufficient to identify the location of the story as the fictional town of Macondo in tropical northern Colombia. The reference to a map hanging in a classroom, 'de un país superpoblado por los excrementos de las moscas' (p.199) is a sardonic sideswipe against conventional representations of a civilized nation. Colombia's history of military uprisings and repression, starting in the late nineteenth century and lasting into the middle of the twentieth, is evoked in separate recollections of civil war (p.199) and the massacre, at a railway station, of banana plantation workers (p. 195) — an event which really happened, in the northern location of Ciénaga, in 1928 (*74*, pp.165–69). All of this information anchors the narrative of 'Un día después del sábado' within precise coordinates of geography and history that are also traced in *La hojarasca*.

As the second-longest story in the volume after 'En este pueblo no hay ladrones', 'Un día después del sábado' is characterised by a relative narrative complexity. Structurally, it offers a variation on the tripartite design of *La hojarasca* (excluding the prologue of that novel), juxtaposing three characters each of whom embodies a particular temperament and mindset: they are a priest, an elderly widow, and a young man from out of town, whose thoughts are exposed, not through the device of an internal focalizer (as in 'Monólogo de Isabel...' or in *La hojarasca*) but through an external, third person narrative viewpoint that moves, like a movie-camera, between the characters and the spaces that define them.

The story opens inside the home of Sra. Rebeca who, on Saturday morning, discovers that the wire-mesh screens on the windows of her house have been damaged. After two paragraphs describing her annoyance and summarising her life and domestic circumstances, the narrative moves out into the town square, where the old widow attempts to register a verbal complaint with the mayor. Attention then shifts to the parish priest, the nonagenarian, Antonio Isabel del Santísimo Sacramento del Altar Castañeda y Montero, whose profound mental distraction and self-absorption prevent him from noticing that the town is being plagued by flocks of birds propelled by a death-wish — 'pájaros rompiendo ventanas para morirse dentro de las casas' (p.185). This disruption in the townsfolk's lives is the work of agents that embody menace and death and has been linked by García Márquez with his reading of Nathaniel Hawthorne (*1*, p.498). At exactly the half-way point of the story, the narrative introduces a young stranger, 'un muchacho apacible' (p.196) who arrives at the town on the afternoon train and books himself into the Hotel Macondo. After the widow and the priest, he occupies the third phase of the narrative, which covers twice as many pages as the earlier introduction of Sra. Rebeca. The three strands eventually come together in a fourth and final section which climaxes with the instruction, given by the priest to the altar boy, Pitágoras, that he collect any eleemosynary monies and give them to the young man from out of town, 'para que se compre un sombrero nuevo' (p.208). By this time, the action has progressed to Sunday morning and now fits the temporal coordinates signalled in the title of the story, 'Un día después del sábado'. That title suggests that everything that happened on Saturday was a prelude to the events of the following day. This is certainly true as far as Sra. Rebeca is concerned: she makes a minimal reappearance in the fourth section of the story, which is dominated by father Antonio Isabel, the outlandish sermon that he delivers on the subject of his encounter with a monstrous figure whom he claims is the Wandering Jew, and his gesture of charity towards the young man. Sections one to three of 'Un día después del sábado', then, appear in retrospect as so many stages in the build-up towards that climactic moment.

iii. The characters

Sections one to three of the story provide pictures of the three major characters that are both colourful and laden with significant detail: in fact, they are painted in a style that will eventually be recognised as typical of García Márquez. Sra. Rebeca, for example, is a member of the Buendía family whose saga will be related in full in *Cien años de soledad*. A 'viuda amargada' who lives alone except for a servant, Argénida, 'su sirviente y confidente desde que murió su esposo', she exemplifies attitudes to property, class and authority that the narrator identifies as part of a criollo heritage: 'La viuda tenía un sentido académico de la autoridad, heredado tal vez de su bisabuelo paterno, un criollo que en la guerra de Independencia peleó al lado de los realistas e hizo después un penoso viaje a España con el propósito de visitar el palacio que construyó Carlos III en San Ildefonso' (p.183). A telling description of the velvet flowers on her sun-hat and her 'zapatos color de plata antigua' (p.184) convey a sense of incongruity and anachronism: like Hawthorne's Hepzibah Pyncheon, Sra. Rebeca belongs to a former age, when her social status granted her certain privileges that are no longer hers to enjoy.[1] Although she now strives to maintain a sense of dignity in the face of adversity, she is prone to embarrassment, cannot avoid lapses into affectation, and is a snob, all of which disposes the reader to disapprove.

The narrative provides other information about Sra. Rebeca's family ties: a distant relative of the local bishop, she is also related to Colonel Aureliano Buendía, who was her first cousin and whom, for whatever reason, she considered 'un descastado'. She was actually married to José Arcadio Buendía, whose death by a single pistol shot inside their home forty years earlier remains an unsolved mystery. In spite of his attempts to use the confessional as a site for drawing her out, father Antonio Isabel has never managed to elicit anything more than 'evasivas' from Sra. Rebeca on the subject of her husband's death, which is elaborated on in section 7 of *Cien años de soledad*. For this and other reasons, he feels ill at ease in her company.

---

[1] *The House of the Seven Gables* (1851) contains a telling sketch, of 'A lady — who had fed herself from childhood with the shadowy food of aristocratic reminiscences [...] this born lady [...] is fain to step down from her pedestal of imaginary rank. [...] Let us behold, in poor Hepzibah, the immemorial lady — two hundred years old, on this side of the water, and thrice as many, on the other — with her antique portraits, pedigrees, coats of arms, records and traditions'. In *The Centenary Edition of the Works of Nathaniel Hawthorne*, 18 vols (Columbus: Ohio State University Press, 1965), vol. II, pp.37–8. According to García Márquez, his reading of *The House of the Seven Gables* 'me marcó por vida' (*1*, p.401) and pre-dated the composition of 'Un día después del sábado' by some five years.

Father Antonio Isabel belongs to an older generation still than Sra. Rebeca — a fact which helps to explain his disassociation from the realities of life in the community. At ninety-four, he is way past his prime and no longer commands any respect or following amongst his parishioners; they veer between ignoring him completely and dismissing him kindly as 'un buen hombre, pacífico y servicial, pero que andaba habitualmente por las nebulosas'. The three paragraphs which introduce the priest use the repetition of the motif of dying birds and 'la habilidad de Satán para filtrarse en el corazón humano por cualquiera de los cinco sentidos' (p.186) as a device to poke fun at him and his peculiar religious ideas. In what follows, his failing mental powers are the object of not one but two jibes by the narrator, who in successive paragraphs remarks first that, 'Para él mismo no habría sido una sorpresa descubrir que estaba muerto [...]', and second, that, 'Sin embargo, él mismo no cayó en la cuenta de que se había vuelto tan sutil en sus pensamientos, que hacía por lo menos tres años que en sus momentos de meditación ya no pensaba en nada' (pp.188–89).

A caricature of senility, father Antonio Isabel functions at one level as an example of that sometimes laughable but ultimately culpable lack of lucidity that blights so many of García Márquez's characters. At another level, and more particularly, he exemplifies the faults in a mindset where religious beliefs merge with madness. The early comedy of the narrator's repeated references to the priest's claims that 'hab[ía] visto al diablo en tres ocasiones' (p.186) shades into a less tolerant assessment of his self-delusion and misconception that reality (the plague of birds) is conforming to one of the narratives of Christian mythology (the myth of the Apocalypse). The priest's visit to Sra. Rebeca's house around *siesta* time on Saturday puts his perception of reality into ironic perspective. Cradling in his hand the form of a bird out of which Sra. Rebeca has just squeezed the last breath, 'se dio cuenta de la prodigiosa verdad que lo rodeaba desde el principio de la semana. Allí mismo [...] asistió a la maravillosa revelación de que sobre el pueblo estaba cayendo una lluvia de pájaros muertos y de que él, el ministro de Dios, el predestinado que había conocido la felicidad

cuando no hacía calor, había olvidado el Apocalipsis' (pp.192–93).
The notions of 'prodigious truth' and 'marvelous revelation', plus
the earnest conviction of playing a privileged part in God's Design,
are held up as exaggerated, misconceived and incongruous with a
reality that, while admittedly extraordinary, is presented through
black humour as being palpably material and base. Also, while there
may be an understandable logic, within a Christian framework, to
the association that the priest makes with the biblical Apocalypse,
that association is immediately emptied of seriousness in the
narrator's comment that, 'Sentado en el escaño de la estación [el
padre] trataba de recordar si había lluvia de pájaros muertos en el
Apocalipsis, pero lo había olvidado por completo'; within seconds,
the priest drifts back into 'sus oscuras nebulosas interiores' (p.193),
which are a constant target of satire in the story.

   Having demonstrated father Antonio Isabel's faltering grasp
on reality, the story intensifies its criticism by allowing for an
exacerbation of the old man's mental state. Insisting, yet again, on
his helpless entanglement in 'una maraña de ideas confusas, entre
las que era imposible diferenciar una sensación nauseabunda y la
pezuña de Satanás atascada en el barro y un tropel de pájaros
muertos cayendo sobre el mundo', it introduces a further term and
arbitrary association into his mental world through the exclamation:
'el Judío Errante' (pp.194–95). This irrational exclamation
confirms beyond the shadow of a doubt that the priest has taken
leave of his senses. When, after a substantial interlude focusing on
the 'muchacho apacible', the narrative turns its attention once more
to the priest, it leaves no room for his rehabilitation in the reader's
eyes. Almost immediately, it inflicts on him an accidental fall to the
ground, which, though pitiable, underscores his lack of sure-
footedness in the physical world. Two paragraphs later, the
narrative follows the priest into the nearly-deserted church and
reports his delivery of a sermon which the townsfolk regard as
further evidence of madness. 'Señora', Argénida tells her mistress,
Rebeca, 'dicen que el padre se volvió loco en el púlpito' (p.206).
Registering this item of hearsay, the story upholds the collective
view against that of the priest: whereas he believes that he is

delivering 'el gran sermón de su vida' (p.205), it is clear that his behaviour is self-indulgent and, as he himself comes to realize, tied up with the sin of pride: 'Por primera vez en su vida, conoció entonces la soberbia' (p.208).

There is, then, little doubt that the principal impulse behind the narrative of 'Un día después del sábado' is towards the exposure of a nonagenarian priest's madness and self-delusion. However, the prevailing mood of the story is sufficiently tolerant and good-humored to allow father Antonio Isabel at least one saving grace. This is manifested at the end of the story through his gesture of generosity towards the young man from Manaure. Whether the result, as Vargas Llosa suggests, of a 'muda complicidad' with a visiting stranger (*28*, p.393), or simply an expression of overwhelming gratitude ('su alma desbordaba gratitud', p.205) for the young man's presence in the almost empty church, the gift to him of monies from the collection compensates for the priest's wild senility, representing, as it does, compliance with the third term of the Christian triptych: hope, faith, and charity. In terms of the alternative code of humanist morality, the priest's gesture demonstrates a sympathetic concern for the welfare of a fellow human being in whose appearance he detects visible signs of neglect and destitution.

iv. The young man from Manaure

Compared with the priest and Sra. Rebeca, the young man from Manaure serves as a vehicle for the exploration of a wider range of human concerns and a focus for examining a set of questions to do with the limits of knowledge and the partiality of our perspectives on the world. The introductory description of 'un muchacho apacible, con nada de particular aparte de su hambre' accords with familiar practices of narrative, as it offers a thumbnail sketch of the young man's character (he is pleasant) and condition (he is hungry). The description is a perfect example of omniscient narration in the realist mode. That style of narration is maintained in the sentences that follow but then becomes problematical in the statement about the young man's entry into the hotel, 'sin ver la tablilla: Hotel

Macondo; un letrero que él no había de leer en su vida' (p.196).
While the narrator has every justification for informing the reader
about the young man's spatial movements, there is a problem with
his telling us that the young man is destined never to read the name-
plate outside the local hotel for as long as he lives. The knowledge
that the narrator displays exceeds the temporal bounds of the setting
of the narrative and is accessible only to a mind or consciousness
that is prescient or even omniscient. Duly alerted to this fact, the
reader wonders why the narrator ruptures the surface of the world of
fiction in so conspicuous a way.

An explanation is to be found in the narrative relationship
between the young man and the priest. The first mention of the
young man announces his arrival in the last carriage of the train as
it pulls into Macondo. Significantly, he is not spotted by the priest,
who at that moment broke a daily habit and 'se alejó de la estación'.
However, the narrative makes a point of telling us that the young
man catches sight of the figure of the priest, from whose presence in
the town he draws an important inference: 'Pensó: "Si hay un cura
debe haber un hotel"'(p.196). At what is a pivotal moment in the
story (we have already acknowledged that the young man's arrival
in Macondo occurs at the physical centre of 'Un día después del
sábado'), the narrative perspective is suddenly reversed, replacing
the point of view of the priest with that of the young man from out
of town, who becomes the focal point of narrative interest over the
next few pages. Through this technical switch, the young man
effectively offers a lure to the reader, who will sympathize with his
predicament and identify with his detached and somewhat bemused
response to characters, situations and events in the town. In truth,
the narrative will return to the perspective of the priest some pages
later, but that does not reduce the structural significance of the
perspective of the young man; on the contrary, the switch back to
the perspective of the priest confirms the importance, within the
narrative system of 'Un día déspues del sábado', of a strategy
involving a contrast between different perspectives on characters
(e.g. the priest), situations (the plague of birds) and events such as
the sermon that father Antonio Isabel eventually delivers to a

congregation including the young man in the final pages of the story.

A good deal of the human interest of 'Un día después del sábado' revolves around the well-drawn figure and agreeable character of the young man, who slips effortlessly into the role of stand-in for the reader. Like us, he is a stranger to the town and a (fictional) human being with as much prior knowledge of Macondo as the readers. Initially, he intends to stay only long enough to eat some food and then resume his journey to an unspecified urban destination. However, a miscalculation leads him to miss the train, investing him with connotations of misfortune and fallibility which facilitate the reader's identification with him, in line with popular wisdom which holds that 'to err is human'. The same may be said about the awkwardness and embarrassment that he feels in the company of the young woman who works at the hotel — feelings that are registered in a sequence of statements constructed cumulatively around a single, significant verb: 'El se sintió mal'; 'Se sentía incómodo'; 'otra vez sintió el pánico por la pérdida del tren'; 'se sintió desconcertado'; and, following a welcome intervention by the hotel owner, 'se sintió menos solo y tuvo deseos de hablar' (pp.197–98). When the narrative accounts for different phases of his life and emphasizes the enduring closeness of the relationship with his mother, the sentimental bond between the young man and his readers grows stronger still. And, when he suddenly realizes that he has left on the train documents entrusted to him by his mother which confirm her entitlement to a pension, the panic and guilt that he feels constitute grounds on which every mother's son can be expected to sympathize with him. As a narrative of human interest, then, 'Un día después del sábado' revolves around this 'muchacho apacible', in ways reminiscent of the neo-realist movies which drew such enthusiastic responses from García Márquez in writings surveyed in Chapter One of this Guide.

In the fourth and final section of the narrative of 'Un día después del sábado', the young man is sutured into the representation of the life of the community in a relatively short passage which shows him having breakfast on the Sunday morning and then walking through the streets of the town to church. García Márquez presents the church cleverly as it comes into the young man's field of vision: 'En este instante desembocó en una pequeña plaza con un edificio de cal con una torre y un gallo de madera en la cúspide y un reloj parado en las cuatro y diez' (p.204). A technique of defamiliarisation is in operation here, involving the mention of four parts of an unnamed whole that together conjure up the idea of a church. It produces an effect that some readers may find comic. Regardless of our response, the narrative incident is bound up in the overall play of perspective that is such an essential part of the grammar of the story. At what is another pivotal moment in the story, the narrative abandons the point of view of the young man for that of the priest in the church. From being the subject of four verbs, the last of which ('penetró') brings him into 'la tibia penumbra de la iglesia casi vacía', the young man becomes the object of a series of three, as he is fixed by the priest's insistent gaze: 'El padre Antonio Isabel [...] iba a iniciar el sermón cuando vio entrar al muchacho con el sombrero puesto. Lo vio examinar con sus grandes ojos serenos y transparentes el templo casi vacío. Lo vio sentarse en el último escaño, la cabeza ladeada y las manos sobre las rodillas' (p.204). From this point on, the narrative shuts out the perspective of the young man. Identifying first with the perceptual field of the priest, it moves laterally to adopt the perspective of Sra. Rebeca and finally comes to rest once more on father Antonio Isabel, whose thoughts and instructions to the altar boy, Pitágoras, bring the narrative to a close. Yet, the structure of shot-reverse shot that has been put in place in the third section of the narrative still exerts a pull on the reader, who is more than well prepared now to imagine the feelings of a self-conscious young man on being singled out for attention by father Antonio Isabel over the course of his extravagant sermon.

From the moment of his introduction, the young man's bemused response to events in the hotel, the streets and the church in Macondo constitutes a viewpoint from which the reader too may observe and evaluate the singular occurrences and the sometimes extraordinary behaviour and attitudes of the characters in 'Un día después del sábado'. If realism entails a form of representation that mimics ordinary modes of perception, then the young man acts as guarantor of the story's realism. This reading contests the view of Frank Dauster that 'it is difficult to find any organic unity' in García Márquez's story (*35*, p.469). Through the character of the young man, 'Un día después del sábado' acquires qualities of realism and a focus of human interest that significantly enrich the depiction of Macondo. In the earliest written of the stories of *FMG*, García Márquez arguably also achieves the fusion of the local and the universal which he praised in his review of 'Un viejo cuento de escopetas' by his fellow Colombian, José Félix Fuenmayor (see above, p.20). The Faulknerian echoes and atmosphere of the town contribute to the delineation of a fictional world that has not only colour and density, but also the dignity ascribed to other, better known locations. This last quality is registered en passant in the story of a 'vicario apostólico' with whom father Antonio Isabel had conversed decades before taking up his ministry in Macondo: described as 'un anciano locuaz e impresionable, aficionado a unos complejos acertijos para eruditos que él decía haber inventado y que se popularizaron años después con el nombre de crucigramas' (p.187), the man concerned exemplifies the cultural worth of those who are deemed to inhabit the periphery. The achievement attributed to him signals the relativity of standards of assessment which accord lesser value to the cultures of the margins than to those of the centre, and presses the claims of the cultures of the Colombian *costa* vis a vis those of the highlands and, indeed, of centres of authority elsewhere. This is a theme which takes on an overtly political inflection in *El coronel no tiene quien le escriba*, in the famous conversation between the colonel and the doctor apropos the Suez crisis of 1956; it also resurfaces in the stories of *FMG* and will necessarily feature again in other sections of this Guide.

'La siesta del martes'

i. Introduction

One of three stories penned in the spring of 1958 (see *73*, p.48), 'La siesta del martes' provides a second, complementary snapshot of Macondo taken from the angle of an outsider who arrives, like the young man from Manaure, on the train. Considerably shorter than the inaugural story of the collection, 'La siesta del martes' effects a significant variation on one of its key themes and structural premises: where 'Un día después del sábado' paid some attention to a son's feelings of love and obligation toward his mother, the subsequent story bears witness to a mother's love for her dead son, positioning her as the principal vehicle of narrative interest and thematic import. A favourite both of the author's and of many of his critics, 'La siesta del martes' condenses universal concerns into a nine-page narrative that stands as a monument to the short story writer's craft.

ii. Narrative style and substance

'La siesta del martes' begins with a description of a train, capturing the precise moment when it 'salió del trepidante corredor de rocas bermejas, penetró en las plantaciones de banano, simétricas e interminables, y el aire se hizo húmedo y no se volvió a sentir la brisa del mar'. The first two verbs convey a lively sense of locomotion and passage from one environment into another, whilst the last two register a sensible change in atmosphere. The precise specification of the banana plantations locates the story in a tropical setting some distance from the coast, as if recorded through the viewfinder of a motion camera. However, the description of the plantations as symmetrical and stretching as far as the eye can see subtly undermines any notion we may have formed that the narrative representation is strictly objective; similarly, the two reflexive verbs 'se hizo' and 'no se volvió a sentir', express a tactile and intelligent response to the changing atmosphere of the landscape. Writing in a style that is quintessentially realistic, García Márquez enhances objective narration by incorporating the sensibility of the observer. Accordingly, in the second sentence of 'La siesta del martes', the activity of narrative observation, now inseparable from physical sensation, is shown to originate inside one of the carriages of the train: 'Una humareda sofocante entró por la ventanilla del vagón'; it is from there that the surrounding landscape is perceived and described in the third and fourth sentences: 'En el estrecho camino paralelo a la vía férrea había carretas de bueyes cargadas de racimos verdes. Al otro lado del camino, en intempestivos espacios sin sembrar, había oficinas con ventiladores eléctricos' (p.119). The impersonal verb 'había', accompanied by a lexicon of concrete nouns imitating exactly the style of Hemingway in the opening paragraphs of 'A Canary for One' (*67*, p.337), affirms a direct equivalence between the world of words and the world of objects as perceived from inside the train.

Having established the narrative and aesthetic foundations of his story, García Márquez now identifies its point of view with two characters who are travelling in the train. They are a mother and daughter, and their circumstances are summed up succinctly in the statement, 'Eran los únicos pasajeros en el escueto vagón de tercera clase' (p.119). The implication that the characters are poor will be confirmed shortly in the observation that the woman 'tenía la serenidad escrupulosa de la gente acostumbrada a la pobreza' (p.120). Before that, the narrative registers the fact that she and her daughter have with them nothing more than 'una bolsa de material plástico con cosas de comer y un ramo de flores envuelto en papel de periódicos' (p.119). A plausible explanation for the foodstuffs and the cut flowers is offered in the comment that the woman and the girl 'guardaban un luto riguroso y pobre' (p.120), prompting the thought that the purpose of their journey is to place the flowers on a grave at an unspecified destination.

The representation of time and space reinforces the pictorial realism of 'La siesta del martes' at this point. Early on, the time is given as 'las once de la mañana' (p.119); some paragraphs later it is after noon ('A las doce había empezado el calor', p.120). The train advances slowly through a number of towns, before eventually drawing into 'un pueblo más grande pero más triste que los

anteriores' (p.121), where it stops and the woman and girl get off;
this happens just before 2 pm and coincides with the 'siesta' of the
town. The narrative immediately supplies an inventory of public
buildings consistent with a small-town environment: 'los
almacenes, las oficinas públicas, la escuela municipal [...], el hotel
frente a la estación, su cantina y su salón de billar, y la oficina del
telégrafo a un lado de la plaza', to which it adds 'la casa cural'
(pp.121–22). The hotel opposite the station provides a link with the
town visited by the young man from Manaure in the earlier story; a
reference just after the mid-point of the present story to Sra. Rebeca
and her 'casa llena de cachivaches' (p.124) clinches its
identification with Macondo.

      The arrival of the mother and daughter in Macondo initiates a
new phase in their story, summarised as follows: exiting the station,
they head immediately to the priest's house, where the mother
wishes to collect the keys to the cemetery in order to place the
flowers on the grave of her son, whom she now identifies as 'Carlos
Centeno Ayala'. He had been shot dead a week earlier by none other
than Sra. Rebeca, when loitering around the back door of her house;
we are not told exactly how the mother and sister came by this
information, since the authorities in Macondo appear not to know
the name 'Carlos Centeno', but the relatives' journey and mourning
are on account of him. At the priest's house, the mother eventually
takes possession of the keys to the cemetery but only after
negotiating a number of obstacles that are placed in her way.
Contrary to most readers' expectations, the story finishes, not by the
side of Carlos Centeno's unmarked grave, but on the threshold of
the priest's house at the moment when the mother and young girl
step out into the glare of the afternoon to face a crowd of local
people who have been awakened from their slumbers and drawn to
the house by the presence of two outsiders.

iii. The heart of the matter

In his analysis of the narrative structure of 'La siesta del martes',
Mario Vargas Llosa suggests that 'El relato fluye hacia un vacío que
el lector tiene que llenar: ese dato escondido es la vivencia principal

de la historia' (*28*, p.352). But such a reading surely misses the point that, by foreclosing on his characters' future, García Márquez deliberately concentrates attention on the fictional present, where the reader can better appreciate the character of the mother and live vicariously the drama of her confrontation with the priest — a confrontation which occupies the core of the narrative and arguably constitutes the most meaningful 'vivencia [...] de la historia'.

The mother of Carlos Centeno has been described by Gene Bell-Villada as 'one of García Márquez's most memorable figures of womanly strength' (*8*, p.121). There is no dispute about his assessment, which has been corroborated by Richard Cardwell, amongst others, in a fine analysis of the author's techniques of characterization (*34*, pp.12–15). By way of illustration, the following short passage typifies the mix of dialogue and commentary that is often used to portray the character of the woman, who is referred to, simply, as 'la mujer':

— Necesito al padre — dijo.
— Ahora está durmiendo.
— Es urgente — insistió la mujer.
Su voz tenía una tenacidad reposada. (p.122)

The laconic speech of the mother conveys her single-minded sense of purpose; her retort to an as yet unnamed interlocutor serves notice that she will not be fobbed off or kept waiting at the doorway of the 'casa cural'. The unaccompanied verb 'insistió' is a master-stroke of economy, a *mot juste* that underlines the fact that this is a woman on a mission. The commentary that follows the dialogue is similarly economical, being both informative and nuanced. It points to a decorum which informs both the moral and the narrative spheres of the story being told. That decorum disposes the reader to respect the character of the mother, her dignified handling of adversity (she has lost her son), and her refusal to dramatize her situation. It also reflects the style of understatement and allusion reminiscent of Hemingway that prevails at the level of the diegesis of the story.

A second exchange, this time with the priest, reveals the mother's moral strength and pride in her son:

— ¿Qué tumba van a visitar? — preguntó [el cura].
— La de Carlos Centeno — dijo la mujer.
— ¿Quién?
— Carlos Centeno — repitió la mujer.

El padre siguió sin entender.

— Es el ladrón que mataron aquí la semana pasada — dijo la mujer en el mismo tono. — Yo soy su madre. (p.124).

Anticipating criticism of her son, the woman answers the priest's questions without hesitation and even takes the initiative by acknowledging that Carlos was a habitual thief — a fact which has not diminished her motherly pride.

A final example demonstrates the immense subtlety of García Márquez's procedures of characterization. It is taken from the last lines of the story, where Carlos Centeno's mother is being asked by the priest and his sister to wait for the afternoon heat to subside before leaving the house. Brushing their concern aside, 'le quitó el ramo de flores a la niña y empezó a moverse hacia la puerta' (p.127). Throughout the story, the bunch of flowers has been held by the daughter and mentioned repeatedly, to the point where it assumes the status of a presiding motif. The flowers are in fact dead, but the daughter still goes for water on the train to revive them. The flowers thus become an ambiguous symbol, of mortality (their life has been cut short, like that of Carlos Centeno) and transcendence (they embody a spiritual desire for revival). By taking them off her daughter, the mother appropriates all of their contradictory symbolism and reaffirms her commitment to her son, on whose grave she must place the flowers in an act of homage.

It is noteworthy that the portrayal of the mother centers almost exclusively round the depiction of her emotional and moral

strength. Apart from these qualities, she exhibits no individuating features. The narrative designates her 'la mujer' throughout, and she identifies herself to the priest as Carlos Centeno's mother: 'Yo soy su madre' (p.124). Rather than her individuality, the narrative emphasizes her typicality and invites the reader to view her as representative of mothers in general. The central episode of her encounter with the parish priest stages a telling confrontation between the mother and a natural code of morality, on the one hand, and, on the other, the value-system of patriarchy, exemplified in the institution of the Catholic Church.

iv. *Mother Right and the Law of the Father*

The concept of 'Mother Right' references a natural morality and standard of justice which Western literature has identified with women, from the time of Sophocles and Euripides down to Brecht, Anouilh and García Márquez. Two foundational texts in this regard are 'Antigone' by Sophocles and 'Suppliant Women' by Euripides. In the play by Sophocles, Antigone challenges the authority of Creon of Thebes, who has given orders prohibiting the burial of the corpses of his defeated political enemies. Amongst the latter is Polynices, who is Antigone's brother. Faced with the dilemma of whether to respect family ties or obey the law of the state, Antigone defies Creon's prohibition and buries Polynices: natural love and loyalty to blood ties override her loyalty to the polis and the patriarchal order. 'Suppliant Women' presents the same story from the angle of the mothers of the dead warriors, represented on the stage by a Chorus of seven women. In the action of the play, their cause is advocated by Aethra, the mother of Theseus, who pleads with him to intercede in favour of the victims. Though initially disinclined to do so, Theseus is provoked by a message from Creon warning him not to interfere in the affairs of Thebes, under threat of retaliation. Embarking on a lengthy and inflated reply, Theseus argues a people's right to self-determination and praises the virtues of democracy over the evils of tyranny. Sensitive, too, to his own reputation in the face of history, he challenges the messenger, 'I am merely asking you [...] to allow the burial of the dead, maintaining the custom of all Greeks. What is improper in this?' (*63*, p.65) and wages a victorious war against Thebes. It is undeniable that his political mediation, military leadership and ingrained male chauvinism detract from the role of the women, who are shown to depend on the decisive intervention of a strong male to correct a human and political injustice. But the moral, as opposed to the political argument that prompts Theseus to act originates in the sensibility of the women, and it is their cause, advocated by Aethra and echoed in the supplications of the seven mothers on stage, that the play holds up as right and worth fighting for.

The placing of a quotation from 'Antigone' at the head of *La hojarasca* (1955) signals a substantial affinity with the work of Sophocles, which García Márquez has commented on in his memoirs. Apparently, when he wrote the novel in the early 1950s he had not yet read 'Antigone' and only did so after Gustavo Ibarra, a literary accomplice, looked over the first draft of *La hojarasca* in 1951 and exclaimed, 'Esto es el mito de Antígona' (*1*, p.473); the quotation from Sophocles was added later, 'como un epígrafe reverencial' (*1*, p.474). Leaving to one side the issue of plagiarism, mentioned with ironic self-deprecation in the same pages of the memoirs, we can affirm categorically that by the time he wrote 'La siesta del martes' at Easter time in 1958, Márquez had read, and possibly re-read 'Antigone'; furthermore, that Sophocles was now an author for whom he professed genuine admiration, but also some anxiety of influence. After *La hojarasca*, the influence of Sophocles and Euripides is felt most strongly in the narration of the encounter between Carlos Centeno's mother and the priest in 'La siesta del martes'.

That episode begins with the mother and daughter being admitted to the 'casa cural', which the priest shares with his sister. Describing the main room, the narrative picks out the following items of décor:

[H]abía una mesa de trabajo, sencilla, con un tapete de hule, y encima de la mesa una máquina de escribir

> primitiva junto a un vaso de flores. Detrás estaban los
> archivos parroquiales. (p.123)

Between them, the typewriter and filing cabinet identify the house
as the space of ritualized bureaucracy. The flowers contained in a
vase next to the typewriter illustrate the assimilation of nature to
culture; they thereby contrast in surroundings and purpose with the
flowers that the mother and daughter are bringing to the grave of
Carlos Centeno.

The formulaic words and, especially, the actions of the priest
on his entry into the room underline his function as chief
bureaucratic officer. The narrative describes how he 'extrajo del
armario un cuaderno forrado de hule, un plumero de palo y un
tintero' (pp. 123–24). He copies the mother's personal details ('los
datos de su identidad') into the register and then returns to the
cupboard, where he keeps the keys to the cemetery. These are
described in close-up as 'dos llaves grandes y oxidadas' and are
elaborated on in a series of matching phrases that undermine the
credibility of the priest: '[eran] como la niña imaginaba y como
imaginaba la madre cuando era niña y como debió imaginar el
propio sacerdote alguna vez que eran las llaves de San Pedro'
(p.125). The passage contrasts the imagination and innocence of
children with the greater scepticism of adults, but faults the priest
for having lost faith long ago in a 'key' symbol of Christianity. The
rusty keys are a fitting image of a belief-system corroded by time
and neglect. They offer a second point of contrast with the bunch of
flowers that the young child is carrying, for, whereas the flowers
symbolize love and hope for revival, the keys, as managed by the
priest in his bureaucratic, custodial capacity, have lost any religious
associations they once had — and should still have — for him.

Edward Waters Hood is right when he observes, 'Es irónico
comparar las llaves del padre con las de San Pedro: las de San Pedro
abren las puertas a la vida eterna, las del sacerdote la puerta del
cementerio, a la muerte eterna' (*29*, p.94). What that critic
overlooks, however, is the story's condemnation of the priest on the
grounds of spiritual laziness and bureaucratic indifference. These

deficiencies come most sharply into focus in the priest's response to the story of Carlos Centeno as told by his mother and sister. Together they explain that Carlos only stole out of need and that the family's poverty even drove him into the boxing ring, where he took repeated beatings and lost all his teeth. The priest's comment, 'La voluntad de Dios es inescrutable', is totally disproportionate to the story of suffering and sacrifice that the mother and daughter have just related to him. The narrator drives the point home by adding that the priest 'lo dijo sin mucha convicción, en parte porque la experiencia lo había vuelto un poco escéptico y en parte por el calor' (p.126).

The designation of the priest throughout as 'el padre' sharpens the story's critique. Ostensibly nothing more than a reflection of social custom in a Catholic community, it in fact emphasizes the priest's role as an agent of patriarchy and of the fathers of the Church. This role and connotation appear in his authoritarian manner towards Carlos's mother and, ironically, in his abject failure to display a surrogate father's love or understanding towards either Carlos or his sister. It is tempting to see the priest's own sister as embodying the virtues of compassion and charity that are conventionally identified with the Mother Church; but her status as a 'mujer soltera' (p.123) rests uneasily with that hypothesis and confirms her more likely significance as merely a servant or hand-maiden in the house of her brother/the Church. Ultimately, she is subject to the Law of the Father embodied in the person of the elderly priest who, in the moral economy of the story, is no match for the values of Mother Right.

v. Broken families and the Christian story

The significance of the family motif in 'La siesta del martes' extends beyond the parameters described above and encompasses other possibilities of meaning and interpretation. The reader will almost certainly have noticed that 'La siesta del martes' is the second story in a row, after 'Un día después del sábado', to feature a family unit downgraded by the absence of the father. In 'Un día después del sábado', the mother entrusts her son with the administration of her pension since she has no husband to do this for her. In 'La siesta del martes', the absence of a pater familias meant that Carlos had to become breadwinner for the family, until he died; in the narrative present, it falls to the mother to perform not only maternal but also paternal roles in caring for her daughter and ensuring that her son is properly buried. In the circumstances, 'behaving properly' means restoring the young man's name, including the patronymic, as well as placing flowers on his grave. The unhelpful attitude of the Church bespeaks a comparative indifference to the hardship endured by the family and reflects the failings of institutionalized patriarchy in the society portrayed.

In addition to its sociological implications, the motif of the family incorporates certain spiritual resonances derived specifically from the Christian story. The evidence for this is understated but persuasive in its consistency. The visit of the mother to her son's grave recalls the presence of the Virgin Mary and Mary Magdalen at the scene of the Crucifixion and invests her with the tragic dignity of a mater dolorosa. A similar undercurrent of loss and sorrow animates the story of the anonymous colonel and his wife, 'huérfanos' of their only son, the Messiah-like Agustín in *El coronel no tiene quien le escriba* (see *64*). In 'La siesta del martes', it is significant that Carlos Centeno 'Era el único varón' (p.125) and willingly brought suffering upon himself so that he might feed his family; indeed, the surname 'Centeno' (rye) identifies him with a basic natural foodstuff and makes him a symbolic 'body-double' of Jesus Christ. This is an association which comes across powerfully in the account of Carlos's death, when he utters the desperate cry, 'Ay, mi madre' (p.125). In addition to their literal sense, his words are redolent of Christ's plea to God during his suffering and convey the sentiment that Carlos has been twice forsaken by the Father: first, by the biological father who abandoned him and his sister, and second, by the symbolic Father standing for institutional indifference and injustice. García Márquez's story about a mother's dignified response to the death of her only son reverberates with a set of associations that are waiting to be activated, at a conscious or semi-conscious level, in the minds of Western and other readers. In

the chapters that follow, we shall have occasion to witness the
suggestive power of Christian archetype in at least one other story in
FMG.

3. A sense of time and place: two stories of the pueblo

'Un día de éstos'

i. La violencia

'Un día de éstos' was the second composition in *FMG*, having been written before March 1958. It preceded 'La siesta del martes' by just a few months and depicted the *pueblo* — an alternative setting which outnumbers Macondo five to three in the collection overall. The stories that follow 'Un día de éstos' and 'La siesta del martes' are all set here, with the exception of 'Los funerales de la Mamá Grande'. According to Dasso Saldívar, the real-life equivalent of the *pueblo* is Sucre, located in the swampy grasslands of the lower Magdalen Basin in northern Colombia. The temporal setting of the stories that take place in the *pueblo* is generally contemporary with the writing, which reverberates with the political violence that erupted in Bogotá in April 1948 and spread throughout the country over the following decade. As recounted by Saldívar, 'la violencia, que colmó el centro y el oriente del país, envió sus ramalazos por el norte hasta los departamentos de Córdoba y Bolívar, especialmente la zona comprendida entre los ríos Cauca y San Jorge, donde se encuentra Sucre. Aunque aquí llegaron no más que eso: ramalazos, el pueblo entró en estado de sitio, y un contingente de policías llegó a finales de 1948 para reforzar el estado de la represión' (*2*, p. 264). This background is evoked in 'Un día de éstos' and 'La viuda de Montiel' and in the novels *El coronel no tiene quien le escriba* and *La mala hora*, where armed forces collude with the local police and capitalist entrepreneurs to terrorise whole communities.

Elaborating on the history of *la violencia* in Sucre, Saldívar uncovers a close and important connection with Márquez's fiction:

> Uno de sus primeros signos realmente preocupantes que
> se percibieron en Sucre fue la llegada de un dentista
> bogotano que se exilió en el pueblo huyendo de la
> encarnizada violencia capitalina. Llegó con una enorme
> depresión, muy resentido con el sistema político de su
> país, y montó su consultorio en el pueblo. García
> Márquez lo conoció bien [...]. Por supuesto, el
> sacamuelas cachaco pasaría a engrosar la lista de sus
> personajes ficticios como el dentista de 'Un día de éstos'
> y de *La mala hora*. (*2*, p. 265)

This account throws light on that part of a writer's creative process
which, in some cases, draws inspiration from real events and
fashions narratives out of empirical data; without exhausting the
possibilities of interpretation and appreciation of a finished product,
it provides a useful starting point for the analysis of 'Un día de
éstos' and its place within *FMG*.

'Don Aurelio Escovar, dentista sin título y buen madrugador'
occupies the centre of a moral and political drama that fills under
four pages in most editions of the story. In respect of plot, Don
Aurelio can be seen as a mirror image of the mother in 'La siesta
del martes', since he is accompanied by his eleven-year-old son and
faces a political opponent, in this case the mayor of the town, who
comes to his surgery on a Monday morning seeking a cure for a
tooth ache. Sandwiched between the sabbath of 'Un día después del
sábado' and the Tuesday of 'La siesta del martes', this story begins
with an introduction to the dentist, his character and place of work,
on a Monday that 'amaneció tibio y sin lluvia' (p.128); the arrival of
the mayor interrupts the dentist's concentration and inaugurates a
central section which culminates in the extraction, without
anaesthetic, of the mayor's damaged tooth; finally, there is a coda,
somewhat shorter than the introduction, which condenses much of
the political sub-text of the story.

Politics form no express part of the introduction, which
sketches a picture of the dentist as meticulous and self-absorbed.
The narrative follows him closely as he takes a mould for false teeth

from a glass cabinet and lays out a set of dentist's instruments, 'como en una exposición'. The narrative registers details of his attire and posture ('era rígido, enjuto') and draws attention to the look in his eye, which it describes as 'una mirada que raras veces correspondía a la situación, como la mirada de los sordos' (p.128). This is an intriguing comment about failure to focus on present circumstances, which conceivably has wider implications than the immediate context of the narrative.

In the next paragraph the story resumes its coverage of the dentist's professional activity and focuses on his polishing the dentures. The attention paid to the dentures in the narrative mimics the dentist's absorption in them and foregrounds them like the bunch of flowers in 'La siesta del martes'. There, the flowers revealed their full significance over the course of the narrative; the reader of 'Un día de éstos' anticipates a similar accretion of sense around the dentures in subsequent sections of the story. For the time being, s/he must proceed on the basis of the available information, which is promptly amplified in a sentence that speculates of the dentist, 'Parecía no pensar en lo que hacía', but adds that 'trabajaba con obstinación' (p.128).

Mention of the advancing time of day and the warming effects of the sun helps to ground the story within a realistic framework. However, two 'gallinazos pensativos' on the ridge of the house next door indicate that another rhetoric is also at work in the story. Buzzards are associated with prey, corpses and death — negative associations which they embody silently and eerily here; the description of them as 'thoughtful' adds a further note of strangeness, since it attributes a human quality to a non-human species, thereby collapsing normal distinctions between categories. In context, the thoughtfulness of the buzzards links thematically with the concentration of the dentist, who 'siguió trabajando con la *idea* (my emphasis) de que antes del almuerzo volvería a llover' and remains immersed '[en] su abstracción' (p.128). The fact that the birds are a pair portends something that cannot be specified as yet.

At this point, four lines of abrupt dialogue interrupt both the narrative rhythm and Don Aurelio's thoughts and split the

introduction of the story in two. The initiator of dialogue is Don
Aurelio's son, who addresses him in the simplest of terms: 'Papá'.
Don Aurelio answers in kind: 'Qué'. The boy continues: 'Dice el
alcalde que si le sacas una muela', and the father replies: 'Dile que
no estoy aquí' (pp.128–29). The role of the son is of interest here.
His presence reflects on his father, who seems to enjoy a close
paternal relationship with his only son; there is no mention of the
mother, who is presumably at home. In spite of the boy's tone (the
narrative refers to his 'voz destemplada', p.128), his presence, like
that of the daughter in 'La siesta del martes', is a guarantee of his
father's humanity.

In the narrative, the son performs the role of intermediary
between his father and the mayor, who has arrived at the surgery
seeking relief from a toothache. The mayor relays his request via the
son, who reports it to his father; the father replies indirectly via the
son. The fact that the mayor is in the waiting room and Don Aurelio
in his surgery, provides a logical explanation for their communicat-
ing via a third party. However, it does not explain why the dentist
tells his son a blatant and audible untruth, which the mayor picks up
on and contests immediately: 'Dice que sí estás porque te está
oyendo' (p.129). This dialogue by proxy continues until the moment
when the mayor exits the waiting room and crosses the threshold
into the surgery, thereby initiating a new phase in the story.

The explanation for the strained relationship between the
dentist and the mayor is provided partly in the dialogue and partly
in the narrative of the second half of the introduction. When the
mayor threatens to shoot the dentist if he does not extract his tooth,
the reader is aware that the phrase 'te pega un tiro' could be a
verbal commonplace uttered out of desperation, but s/he then
realises that the reference to a firearm is serious and potentially
loaded: in the space of a few seconds, the narrative shows the
dentist calmly opening a drawer where he keeps a real revolver. It is
the presence of this handgun that encourages him to tell his son:
'Dile que venga a pegármelo' (p.129). This comment and situation
point to a historical relationship of antagonism between the dentist
and the mayor. What is more, the presence of a gun in the dentist's

surgery raises the question, why is it there? By way of an answer, the reader supposes an air of lawlessness about the *pueblo*, originating in the political climate of the town and surrounding region. In the first page and a half of his story, García Márquez thus sets the scene of *la violencia* as backdrop to the meeting that takes place between a small-town dentist and a mayor who, though momentarily vulnerable, personifies a threat to life.

The introduction to 'Un día de éstos' contains a further semiotic element, which thickens its texture of suggestion. This is 'un diente de oro' (p.129) that Aurelio polishes with almost infinite patience and dedication. The tooth is described in two brief paragraphs interleaved between the mayor and the dentist's reported speech. Initially a theatrical prop, it assumes a dramatic role by providing the means through which the dentist keeps the mayor waiting; for the dentist, the value of the tooth is therefore not only tactical but also psychological, as it momentarily gives him the upper hand in a power struggle. The fact that it is made out of gold increases the tooth's association with resistance, since gold has the reputation of being a material that is especially strong and durable. This property combines with the more common connotation of gold as a precious metal to enhance the symbolic capital of the dentist, whose name, 'Aurelio', makes him the personification of all of its prized qualities.

ii. Political payback

The central section of 'Un día de éstos' develops the dramatic and symbolic potential of the introduction into a political narrative of skilfully managed tension and double entendres. By placing himself in the hands of the dentist, the mayor cedes power to him and becomes, for a moment, vulnerable. The situation of the two men is in fact redolent throughout of a scenario of torture and sadism, with the tables being turned in favour of the (normally) weaker, victimized party. Significantly, the narrative identifies the mayor with the military through a number of details: he wears a 'guerrera' (p.131) and salutes in military style; most pointedly, the dentist addresses him as 'teniente', thus evoking the contemporary situation in Colombia and elsewhere in Latin America, where power rested with the military or paramilitary. The dentist, for his part, has the mayor at his mercy and, if he wished, could behave like one of the monsters of sadism pictured in films such as 'Marathon Man' (dir. John Schlesinger, 1976) or, more topically, in literary works on the theme of 'los desaparecidos' in Latin America. In fact, he does act vengefully towards the mayor, first, by operating without anaes-thetic under the pretext that the mayor's tooth is affected by an abscess, and, second, by telling the mayor, as he extracts the tooth with a twist of the wrist, 'Aquí nos paga veinte muertos, teniente' (p.130). The moment of payback anticipated in the story's title acquires its most eloquent dramatisation here, with the dentist wrenching the tooth out of the mayor's lower gum, to the accompaniment of the cited words.

However, in spite of having an opportunity to inflict vicious and disproportionate pain on a political opponent, the dentist resists and is even shown as exercising a measure of sensitivity and care towards his patient. The narrative comments on how Don Aurelio handles the mayor's jaw at the end of the preliminary examination, 'con una cautelosa presión de los dedos'. He attends to all of the requirements of hygiene, including the sterilisation of his dental instruments. Most significantly, at the moment when he might be expected to vent hatred on the mayor, he addresses him 'sin rencor, más bien con una amarga ternura' (p.130), as he tells him that he is avenging the deaths of twenty of his political comrades. The restraint and lack of rancour felt by the dentist make of him a complex character who avoids the trap and temptation of duplicat-ing the excesses committed by his political enemies in the period of institutionalized violence that overran Colombia from 1948 on.

Having built up to the extraction of the mayor's tooth, the narrative allows dramatic tension to subside some twenty lines before the end of the story and concentrates its attention on other things. The first object that comes into view is the mayor's extracted tooth, which is spotlighted in two sentences as follows: '[el alcalde] la vio a través de las lágrimas. Le pareció tan extraña a su dolor que no pudo entender la tortura de sus cinco noches anteriores' (pp.130–

31). The narrative stresses the mayor's perception of his tooth and his sense that it has nothing to do with the experience of pain suffered over a period of five days and their respective nights. The political overtones of the term 'tortura' are nonetheless clear to the reader and chime in with the climate of violence that is the background to the story. The combination of torture and insensitivity is especially disturbing, since it suggests a morally corrupt and inhuman environment.

The tooth, once removed, stands out in isolation and invites interpretation. In the thematic structure of the story, it is linked with damage and pain. In relation to other symbols, it refers back to the gold tooth mentioned at an earlier stage of the narrative and emerges as a counter-motif: whereas the gold tooth was associated with durability and resistance, the extracted tooth is decayed to its core. The political symbolism requires no fleshing out: the cause of Aurelio and his comrades, many of them dead, has greater value than the cause of the mayor and his accomplices. Aurelio and his band also represent a set of moral values that outshine those of the opposition, who are corrupt. Unfortunately, the prospects for resistance and success are not good for Aurelio and his comrades: after all is said and done, the mayor and his accomplices remain in power and will continue to run the town. But the indestructible germ of resistance will persist.

The moral and political outlook for the *pueblo* is captured in a complex image of 'una telaraña polvorienta con huevos de araña e insectos muertos' hanging against the background of a cloudless sky. Reminiscent of the pair of buzzards mentioned earlier, the spider's web symbolises the dominant and self-perpetuating order of corruption and death in the town, where victims fall into a predator's net — as happens to the colonel in a tense moment in *El coronel no tiene quien le escriba*, for example. But the wider horizon is perceptibly brighter. Caught inextricably in the web of political repression, the dentist in García Márquez's story is combating arachnid opposition, against which he scores a significant victory. That victory is small-scale and temporary, as critics such as Bell-Villada and Williams have rightly insisted,

pointing to the restoration of power relations at the end of the story
(*8*, p.123 & *30*, p.53). There, the dentist asks the mayor whether he
should bill him directly for his services or send the bill to the town
hall, for it to be paid out of public funds. The mayor's reply, 'Es la
misma vaina' (p.131), bespeaks his total lack of scruples about
paying a personal debt out of the public purse. Having ceded power
briefly to the dentist, the mayor now resumes his position of
unaccountability in the town, justifying a negative reading of the
story and its outcome. However, that would involve overlooking the
stubborn symbolism of the gold tooth, which permeates Aurelio's
surgery and reflects onto his person. The abiding message of 'Un
día de éstos' seems to be that in a regime dominated by *la violencia*
and its associated corruption, resistance has a value that cannot be
prized enough. As durable as gold, it represents an exemplary
standard of political morality, to which Aurelio will continue to
adhere this day and hereafter.

'La prodigiosa tarde de Baltazar'

i. Introduction

The picture of the town conveyed in 'Un día de éstos' acquires a
fuller outline in 'La prodigiosa tarde de Baltazar', through a cast
which features the thirty-year-old eponymous carpenter-artisan, who
for the past four years has been living with Ursula 'sin casarse y sin
tener hijos' (p.165); a doctor, Don Octavio Giraldo, representing the
professional middle classes, and his invalid wife; and the rich José
Montiel, commonly called 'don Chepe', married to a neurotic
woman 'torturada por la obsesión de la muerte' (p.169) and mother
of his twelve year old son. The mention of not one but three
heterosexual couples sets this story apart from the previous triad,
where only one parent was in evidence per story. The presence of a
child carries over from both 'La siesta del martes' and 'Un día de
éstos', and adumbrates greater 'normality' in family relations;
however, this is no guarantee of a healthy domestic life, as the
neurosis and sickness found in the homes of (ironically) the doctor
and (more predictably) the Montiels, testify.

A key difference from 'Un día de éstos' is the absence of any direct allusion to political violence in 'La prodigiosa tarde de Baltazar'. Instead, the emphasis of the narrative falls on the characters and their different responses to an extraordinary object which makes an extraordinary impact on the *pueblo*: this is a bird cage, made over the course of a long and troubled fortnight by Baltazar, which becomes the focus of desire, debate and disagreement over questions of value, truth, morality, social conflict, and art. As the hub of so many concerns, it is not surprising that the bird cage suffices as the story's sole motif, without the need for any accompanying prop to contest or complement it.

The title 'La prodigiosa tarde de Baltazar' is one of just three in the collection to name the story's central character (the others being 'La viuda de Montiel' and 'Los funerales de la Mamá Grande'). This casts some retrospective light on the first three stories of the collection and confirms the proportionally greater narrative and thematic prominence of social over personal concerns in them. Naturally, this is not to detract from the individual profiles of characters such as father Antonio Isabel, the mother of Carlos Centeno, or Aurelio Escovar, all of whom stick in the memory by reason of a personal eccentricity or peculiar strength. Rather, it is to highlight a strategy, opted for by the author, which underlines the role of a particular character in a particular narrative design; a strategy which also predisposes the reader of 'La prodigiosa tarde de Baltazar' towards a hermeneutic approach which assumes the eponymous character's centrality and relatively greater significance in the story than, say, his partner, Úrsula, or Pepe, the twelve-year-old son of the Montiels.

Another element in the title that colours the reader's expectations is the 'prodigiosa tarde' which we anticipate will frame the narrative of Baltazar. The adjective and, especially, its unusual placing before the noun prepare us to read about an afternoon or evening in the character's life which will be distinguished by some extraordinary characteristic, experience or event(s). Already applied, with satirical intent, to father Antonio Isabel's musings in 'Un día después del sábado' (p.192), the epithet 'prodigioso/a' connotes,

in addition to the extraordinary, the marvellous and the miraculous
— categories which in turn presuppose a standard and a
hermeneutic perspective from which to evaluate instances of those
categories.

ii. Narrative structure and plot

The events of the narrative of 'La prodigiosa tarde de Baltazar' in
fact exceed the limits of an afternoon and/or evening, lasting from
just before lunch time on an unspecified working day in April,
through dusk and midnight to 5 o'clock the following morning.
Baltazar's prodigious experiences evolve through four narrative
stages of which the first three fit within the time-frame of the title;
interestingly, the final stage exceeds it.

As the story opens, the narrative gives equal prominence to
Baltazar and the birdcage that has taken him two weeks to produce:
'La jaula estaba terminada. Baltazar la colgó en el alero, por la
fuerza de la costumbre [...].' The second adverbial clause indicates
that, as far as Baltazar is concerned, he has done nothing out of the
ordinary in producing the birdcage. The narrator subsequently
clarifies that the only difference vis a vis Baltazar's normal working
practices is a difference of degree: 'Para él, acostumbrado a hacer
jaulas desde niño, aquel había sido apenas un trabajo más arduo que
los otros' (p.165).

Baltazar's lack of awareness characterises him from the outset
as a naïf and as one who, in spite of having turned thirty, is not
entirely attuned to the world around him. The narrative glosses the
point, informing us that, 'la vida le había dado muchos motivos
para estar alerta, pero ninguno para estar asustado'. And yet, while
definitely not '[un] muchacho asustado' (p.165), he seems to be
anything but alert. However, compensation for this deficiency is at
hand in the person of his partner, Úrsula, who provides a framework
of order and practicality in their lives. It is Úrsula who, overcoming
her annoyance at the amount of time that Baltazar has spent
producing the cage, asks him how much he intends to charge for it.
Comparing it with other cages he has made in the past, she says he
should charge according to the amount of time invested and the size

of the product; she even suggests a guide price and identifies a likely purchaser, don Chepe Montiel.

Úrsula occupies an interesting position in the world of domestic and social relations portrayed in the story. On the one hand, she compensates for Baltazar's lack of nous and looks after the interests of the home. On the other, she acts as a buffer between the household and society, where the birdcage makes a huge impact. By the time she and Baltazar have finished lunch, the birdcage is on everybody's lips and indeed, 'ya se decía por todos lados que era la jaula más bella del mundo' (p.165). It is this knowledge that prompts Úrsula to pay serious attention to the cage and to form a view of it, which she does in terms of size and value, rather than beauty: 'es bien grande. Creo que es la jaula más grande que he visto en mi vida' (p.166).

News of the birdcage brings hordes of people to Baltazar and Úrsula's house, including the local doctor, Octavio Giraldo. His arrival initiates the second stage of the narrative and converts the birdcage into an object, first, of inflation and then, of dispute. As soon as he hears about it, the doctor is interested in acquiring the cage for his invalid wife, and he comes to see it on his way back from visiting a patient at home. A careful examination persuades him that 'en efecto, aquella jaula era superior a su propio prestigio, y mucho más bella de lo que había soñado jamás para su mujer'; praising it as 'una aventura de la imaginación', he tells Baltazar, 'Hubieras sido un extraordinario arquitecto' (p.167) and offers to buy the cage there and then.

The doctor's evaluation is a crucial step in the process whereby the cage acquires public value as an object that is marketable, as well as beautiful. The suggestion that Baltazar could have been an architect also contributes to the cage's rhetorical inflation, as noticed by Eduardo González (*41*, pp.18–19). The reader cannot remain detached from this spiral of appreciation, since s/he views the birdcage from the same vantage point as the doctor. On display in the dining-room, the cage offers itself for examination, and there is no better-qualified professional to carry out that task than the doctor:

Puesta en exhibición sobre la mesa, la enorme cúpula de
alambre con tres pisos interiores, con pasadizos y
compartimientos especiales para comer y dormir, y
trapecios en el espacio reservado al recreo de los
pájaros, parecía el modelo reducido de una gigantesca
fábrica de hielo. El medico la examinó cuidadosamente
[…]. (p. 167)

The image of the cage is built up through a set of terms that call to
mind a monument such as a church ('cúpula'), spaces of domesticity
('compartimientos para comer y dormir'), and the circus ('trapecios'). An otherwise functional object is thereby invested with a
wealth of associations that are further enhanced by the comparison
of the cage to a miniature ice factory: connotations of industry and
refreshment (especially welcome in the tropical heat) combine in the
final simile with a strong visual impression of the beautiful airiness
and luminosity of the cage, whose wire structure resembles the lines
that are refracted in a block of ice. The cage is thus constructed as
the site of a surplus of meanings, as well as an object of beauty.

Doctor Giraldo's offer to purchase the cage complicates the
story-line, for no sooner has he spoken than Úrsula informs him that
'[la jaula] está vendida'; Baltazar explains that he made it for Pepe
Montiel, who 'la mandó a hacer expresamente'. Whereas Baltazar's
words are confirmed as true some pages later, there is some
ambiguity about Úrsula's assertion. In practice, all she has done is
to advise Baltazar to ask for sixty pesos for the cage, which she has
told him don Chepe Montiel can easily afford; but she has not
clinched any deal. Her assertion that the cage 'Está vendida' (p.167)
is true only to the extent that she has a buyer in mind and no longer
regards the cage as being for sale. This ambiguity hangs over the
ensuing conversation with the doctor, who first attempts to persuade
Baltazar that the cage he has made is not necessarily the cage he
was asked to make, and then tries to force the issue by declaring that
he must take the cage home with him now because he already
promised it to his wife 'para esta tarde' (p.168). We cannot verify

this claim and have reason to suspect that the doctor is raising the stakes in order to put moral pressure on Baltazar.

If that is his strategy, then it fails. Baltazar brings the discussion to a close, saying semi-apologetically, 'Lo siento mucho, doctor [...] pero no se puede vender una cosa que ya está vendida' (p.168). Baltazar's witty remark shows that he is, in fact, a dialectical match for the wily, insistent doctor. Yet, it also shows Baltazar locking himself into the position staked out by Úrsula and effectively closing off any possibility of selling the cage to the doctor. García Márquez displays acute psychological insight throughout this episode, which ends with Baltazar silently leaving it up to Úrsula to answer the doctor's question as to how much he has been paid for the cage. Her answer, 'Sesenta pesos' (p.169), is consistent with her earlier advice, but is in fact a lie, since neither she nor Baltazar has received any money for the cage. This is something that Baltazar must know only too well. His embarrassment and reticence in the company of a forceful woman are perhaps understandable, but his acquiescence in a rhetorical falsehood is less easy to explain away.

The following stage of the narrative restores Baltazar's image by pitting him against the local capitalist, Montiel, and granting him a resounding moral victory over an opponent who is shown to lack humanity, generosity of spirit, and self-control. The description of Baltazar as he arrives at Montiel's house spells out the terms on which the two men will figuratively do battle, namely: poor vs. rich, innocence vs. cynicism, and cleanliness vs. slovenliness. Baltazar arrives 'vestido de blanco y acabado de afeitar, con esa expresión de decoroso candor con que los pobres llegan a la casa de los ricos' (p.169). The narrative elaborates, 'Nunca se sintió bien entre los ricos. Solía pensar en ellos, en sus mujeres feas y conflictivas, en sus tremendas operaciones quirúrgicas, y experimentaba siempre un sentimiento de piedad' (p.170). The adjectives in this final sentence betray the subjective basis of Baltazar's view of the rich, but the concluding reference to 'un sentimiento de piedad' reflects admirably on him as the embodiment of a key quality of the human spirit.

In its coverage of Baltazar's meeting with Montiel, the narration highlights selected details of the latter's physical appearance which contrast sharply with that of Baltazar. Montiel is 'corpulento y peludo' and he enters the dining room from his bedroom 'en calzoncillos' (p.170), not having had sufficient time to bathe or dress. The contrast with the white-clad Baltazar's aura of hygiene and propriety could hardly be greater. The narrative then considers Montiel's relations with his wife and son and mentions the air of 'quieto patetismo' that is common to them both. An explanation is provided immediately in the scene of Montiel's bullying of Pepe, whose hair he pulls, and the cowed whisper in which Adelaida begs him to refrain from hurting their son. The scene is thus set for the brutal and insensitive Montiel to pick up the cage from the dining-room table 'sin mirarla' and place it in Baltazar's hands, with the order that he should remove it from the house and find a buyer elsewhere; he also admonishes Baltazar for having acted on Pepe's instructions without conferring with him directly. In spite of the overwhelmingly negative thrust of Montiel's characterisation, it is hard to quibble with his reasoning here: Baltazar took the commission from a twelve-year-old boy who is technically under age, and Montiel has every right to upbraid Baltazar with having gone behind his back and contracted 'con un menor' (p.171).

However, the narrative is not inclined to favour Montiel over Baltazar. Affected by the sight of Pepe throwing a tantrum of disappointment and (in all likelihood, simulated) rage, Baltazar presents him with the cage, 'sonriendo', and tells him, 'Quédate con ella'. Montiel objects, 'No seas tonto, Baltazar. Llévate tu trasto para la casa y no hagas más tonterías'; he also emphasizes that 'No pienso pagarte ni un centavo'. However, Baltasar counters, 'No importa. La hice expresamente para regalársela a Pepe. No pensaba cobrar nada' (p.172), and makes ready to leave the house by the front door. The story thus reaches a dramatic climax, with Montiel bellowing insults at a departing Baltazar who would appear to have scored an important moral victory over him.

In an enlightening study of 'La prodigiosa tarde de Baltazar', Eduardo González has linked the eponymous character's gesture of generosity to the phenomenon of gift-exchange in primitive societies (*41*). Although not widely recognized by the story's commentators, Baltazar's name marks him out as a bearer of gifts: along with Gaspar and Melchor, Baltasar was one of the three Wise Men who brought gifts to the baby Jesus at the Nativity. In our own times, the 'Reyes Magos' continue to fulfil a prominent role in the Catholic ritual of Christmas and Epiphany in Spanish-speaking countries and elsewhere. In the context of García Márquez's narrative, Baltazar's gesture of generosity occurs significantly at the moment when 'Úrsula, en su casa, cantaba una canción antigua, mientras cortaba rebanadas de cebolla' (p.172). An aura of archetype thus envelops the episode and invests Baltazar's gift of the cage with a prodigious quality.

It is noteworthy that critics have been far from unanimous in their reading of this episode. For Bell-Villada, Baltazar's gift of the cage to Montiel junior is a triumph (*8*, p.124), whereas for D.W. Foster it is an ignominious surrender — of personal dignity as well as of financial capital (*37*, pp.40–43). More circumspectly, George McMurray saw 'paradox and ironic ambiguity' at work in the text (*20*, p.57) and anticipated Eduardo González's later opinion, that Baltazar's gift of the cage 'seems to be at once ridiculous and magnificent' (*41*, p. 23). A sense of complexity certainly informs the event and needs to be acknowledged in our response to it.

Much depends on how we interpret Baltazar's claim that he had not intended to charge anything for the cage ('No pensaba cobrar nada', p.172). Such a claim reflects faithfully the artisan's initial indifference to monetary considerations relating to the birdcage. However, it is inconsistent with his and Ursula's subsequent musings about what would be a fair price to charge; inconsistent, too, with the figure of 60 pesos mentioned to the doctor just a few minutes before Baltazar leaves home and walks the short distance to Montiel's house. McMurray's thesis with regard to 'the ascendancy of paradox and ironic ambiguity' in the reader's mind (*20*, p.57) is borne out by this moment in the plot of 'La tarde prodigiosa de Baltazar'. However, it is also fair to assert that Baltazar's moral strength outweighs by far any moral weakness at this point. We remember his acquiescence in the telling of a lie to the doctor; and we concede that his statement to Montiel, 'No pensaba cobrar nada', may be a cowardly backing down, but his gesture of generosity still shines through and gains favour with the reader, who takes delight in the discomfiting of Montiel.

The theory of gift-exchange helps to clarify the extent of Baltazar's moral and psychological victory over Montiel (whose surname characterises him as a mountain of ice or bile). According to Marcel Mauss, gift-exchange is an ancient institution which demands reciprocity. Receiving and giving a gift in return binds the primitive group together, and failure to reciprocate according to this simple code threatens to rupture the bond that unites society. Being put in a position where one is unable to reciprocate is especially embarrassing, since one feels beholden to the other. An outburst by Montiel at the end of the third section of 'La prodigiosa tarde de Baltazar' illustrates this particular stress-point, perfectly. Watching as Baltazar leaves his house and the cage behind, Montiel shouts after him, 'Estúpido. Llévate tu cacharro. Lo único que faltaba es que un cualquiera venga a dar órdenes en mi casa. ¡Carajo!' (p. 172). Apropos this passage, Eduardo González observes of Montiel, 'On the social plane he fears the rupture of hierarchy in the feeling of being beholden' (*41*, p. 21). His dismissal of Baltazar as 'un cualquiera' bespeaks the local capitalist's acute discomfort at being bested, as he sees it, by a social inferior. What is more, the final expletive, as well as releasing some of Montiel's pent-up rage, exposes a certain vulnerability in respect of his masculinity, which feels threatened by the prodigious generosity of a minion who up to that point had served only 'para hacer trabajos de carpintería menor' (p. 170) in his home.

A more nuanced and problematical perspective on moral issues emerges in the fourth and final stage of the narrative of 'La prodigiosa tarde de Baltazar'. The setting shifts to the local billiard saloon, where the people of the town welcome Baltazar with an ovation. They have heard about his confrontation with Montiel from a bunch of 'curiosos' who witnessed it, and they now treat him as a local hero who has won a rare and precious victory over the rich and powerful Montiel. However, they base their exalted view of Baltazar on information which is incorrect, since they believe that he has successfully sold the cage to Montiel, for the sum of 50 pesos. The people's rapturous reception has a peculiar effect on Baltazar, which the narrative highlights in two crucial sentences:

Hasta ese momento, pensaba que había hecho una jaula mejor que las otras, que había tenido que regalársela al hijo de José Montiel para que no siguiera llorando, y que ninguna de esas cosas tenía nada de particular. Pero luego se dio cuenta de que todo eso tenía una cierta importancia para muchas personas, y se sintió un poco excitado. (pp.172–73)

The reader can sympathise with Baltazar and understand his reaction to the crowd. However, s/he cannot be quite so understanding about the apparent insouciance with which Baltazar says that he has been paid 60, not 50 pesos for the cage. Earlier, he had remained silent when Ursula told the doctor that they had received 60 pesos for it; now, it is he who makes a false statement and plays along with the popular pretence that he has done something heroic that calls for a celebration. As a result, his moral capital begins to diminish. He gets drunk and fantasizes about 'un fabuloso proyecto de mil jaulas de a sesenta pesos, y despúes de un millón de jaulas hasta completar sesenta millones de pesos', which he imagines wresting from 'los ricos antes que se mueran'. Whereas the story at an earlier juncture has given rhetorical support to the poor against the rich, Baltazar's attitude here is vitiated both by a lack of realism in his vision and by the telling description of him as 'ciego de la borrachera' (p.173) — where blindness contradicts the highly-prized value of lucidity. In the circumstances, Baltazar's drunkenness reaches extremes that are first, ridiculous, and then almost pitiful: abandoned by his admirers, he ends up in the street, vaguely aware that someone is stealing his shoes, but still clinging to what for him is 'el sueño más feliz de su vida'. The story concludes with the notice that 'Las mujeres que pasaron para la misa de cinco no se atrevieron a mirarlo, creyendo que estaba muerto' (p.174), which shows how far his stock has fallen in the people's eyes.

iii. Critical opinion and strategies for interpreting 'La prodigiosa tarde de Baltazar'

Critical opinion is as polarized over the conclusion of the story as it was over Baltazar's act of giving the cage to Pepe Montiel. For David W. Foster, at one extreme, 'the closing words of the text [...] underline the disaster that [Baltazar's] work of art has brought him'; indeed, '[his] degeneration could not be more complete' (*37*, p.41). At the other, Gene Bell-Villada proclaims that 'The generosity of Baltazar ultimately carries the day [...]. Though he ends up drunk in the gutter, minus his wrist watch and shoes, he has had his moment of glory, complete with cheering crowds and women's kisses' (*8*, p.124). In the light of our analysis, Foster's reading errs in giving no credit whatsoever to Baltazar, whom it sees as the object of a remorselessly ironic demystification and as a self-deluding fool. Such a view, crucially, denies Baltazar any nobility in giving the birdcage away to Pepe Montiel; also, it cannot accommodate the positive significance of Baltazar's embarrassment of Montiel, as interpreted by Eduardo González with the aid of the theory of 'gift-exchange'.

Bell-Villada's reading is more inclusive than Foster's. What is particularly interesting about it is the way that he resolves the undeniable tension(s) between positives and negatives in García Márquez's characterization of Baltazar. Bell-Villada concedes Baltazar's final ignominy but sees it as being eclipsed by the earlier virtue of generosity. In the process, he assumes an overarching unity where in fact there have been many ironies and complexities in Baltazar's behaviour. To a lesser degree than Foster, Bell-Villada still does violence to the story by seeking to subsume it under a totalizing interpretation.

Considering alternative strategies for accounting for the diverse reactions and instincts of Baltazar, we might entertain the hypothesis of an adult male, somewhat out of touch with day to day realities and dependent (like other male characters in the Márquez oeuvre) on a woman to anchor him in the 'real' world; a man who is rather weak of will, to the point of being suggestible and inclined to go with the flow, even if this entails acquiescing in another person's half-truths or telling white lies oneself; and, finally, a man so careless with himself that he takes part for the first time ever in a drinking binge that ends in the gutter and in a semi-conscious state where he is persuaded, nonetheless, that he is living 'el sueño más feliz de su vida'. This tolerant, even permissive reading would approximate at many points to the character and story of Baltazar, but at the cost of reducing him to some kind of bland non-entity. It would replace one or other of Foster or Bell-Villada's readings of Baltazar with another totalizing reading that would ultimately be no more satisfying or nuanced than theirs.

A second strategy derives its rationale from the close analysis of the narrative of 'La prodigiosa tarde de Baltazar', conducted in the present pages. This strategy would underline Baltazar's shifting moral stance and not seek to downplay his final lapse into dishonesty, drunkenness and irresponsibility. It would, however, stress the earlier predominance of positive over negative factors in Baltazar's motivation and preserve unsullied the story's claim that he should be recognized for having achieved something miraculous over the course of a special afternoon and evening. This reading would distinguish between the different messages conveyed in the different stages of the narrative and separate out the fourth and final stage, on the grounds that it does not fall within the bounds of '[una] prodigiosa tarde'. Clearly, the events of nightfall and early morning follow organically on from those of stages one to three, making it impossible to divorce them from the 'prodigiosa tarde de Baltazar'; they tarnish the image of Baltazar, without a doubt. But, on the reading being proposed here, they do not cancel out the eponymous character's earlier heroics: rather, they complement the kindness, positive lack of ego, and anti-authoritarian instinct that

Baltazar displayed at the climax of stage three. This means that Baltazar appears as less integral a character than Aurelio Escovar or the mother of Carlos Centeno; but it does not mean that he is a shameless coward or a hypocrite, for example. His moral and intellectual weaknesses place him in the category of fallible human beings, represented by the priest in 'Un día después del sábado' or the young man from Manaure in the same story, who commits a single error — little more than a lapse of concentration — at one fateful moment in his journey to the town where he was supposed to secure his mother's pension.

Amongst the consequences of the strategy just described is an obligation on the reader to recognise the story's rhetorical operations and discriminate between its dissonant perspectives of sympathy towards, and judgement on the main character. David W. Foster and Raymond Williams place considerable emphasis on the text's construction of a variety of fictionalized readers, amongst which they privilege a narrataire who enjoys a relationship of complicity with the author and shares an ironic perspective on the fictional world and characters of 'La prodigiosa tarde de Baltazar'. The light that these two critics shed on the workings of the narrative is considerable. However, the tendency, especially in the case of Foster, to resolve contradiction into monolithic synthesis indicates the need for the reader to respect a complementary principle, which is the avoidance of dogmatism. Espoused by Eduardo González (*41*, p. 30), this principle is inscribed in the text itself, through the shifting stages of the narrative and, signally, through the over-determined image of the birdcage, which is a model of openness to interpretation: light and airy within its sturdy wire frame, it awakens varying responses in individuals of different social classes and ages and ultimately resists interpretive closure.

The aura that surrounds the birdcage identifies it not just as a thing of beauty, which it is for virtually all the characters except Úrsula and Montiel, but also as a paradigmatic work of art. Vargas Llosa reduces García Márquez's story essentially to a conflict between imagination (Baltazar) and brute reality ('lo real objetivo') (*28*, p. 377), whilst Raymond Williams interprets it as 'a statement about society and the artist's role in it' (*30*, p.50). In the opening paragraphs, Baltazar fits the type of the artist whose inspiration distracts him from the prosaic world of domestic relations and money; the carpenter-artisan simply cannot gauge the financial worth of the birdcage he has made, and he must rely on Úrsula to put a price on it. The conflicts that ensue, first with the doctor and then with Montiel, are an object lesson in the discrepancy that arises between labour value and cash value under the capitalist system. Perhaps more pointedly, the story illustrates the alienation of the artisan from the product of his labour, a point made, not without some bitterness, in the recounting of Baltazar's drunken speculation about reproducing his cage a million-fold — an action which would, of course, destroy the unique aura of the original, a million times over.

There may an allegory here of the fate that awaits any work of art once it enters the public domain. Cut loose from its creator (in this case, Baltazar) and hung up on display (as happens in the opening paragraph of the story), the cage 'becomes a tuning fork which registers the resonances of each individual's perception of it' (*41*, p.19). At the social level, the cage becomes a battlefield for competing evaluations and claims on it — both within and outside the bounds of the text. Gifted to Pepe, the cage still unsettles Montiel *père* and then, shortly after, gives the common people cause to celebrate. Yet, by the end of the story it has disappeared from view, replaced by the drunken form of Baltazar, who lies on the street, penniless and owing a considerable debt, the embodiment, possibly, of a cautionary tale. Meanwhile, outside the world of the story, 'La prodigiosa tarde de Baltazar' circulates freely both in the commercial realm and amongst the legions of critics of García Márquez's work. The existing variety of readings of 'La prodigiosa tarde de Baltazar' is testimony in part to the wealth of meanings that the story has been capable of generating to date; more than forty years after the original date of publication and over twenty five since David W. Foster penned his historic essay on it, the story continues to resonate with critics and general readers, who respond to its prodigious aura with undiminished interest and pleasure.

4. 'En este pueblo no hay ladrones':
the battered woman and her beau

i. Introduction

This, the longest story in the volume, adds considerably to the sociological and topographical depiction of 'the town' already provided in 'Un día de éstos' — composed around the same time as 'En este pueblo no hay ladrones' — and 'La prodigiosa tarde de Baltazar', which followed a few months later. In the larger scale of its portrayal, the town acquires features including a river and jetty similar to those frequented by the colonel in *El coronel no tiene quien le escriba*; a hotel and cinema, where the film showing on one of the many nights of the story stars the popular Mexican actor, Cantinflas; a number of shops and a bustling Sunday market; a seedy dance-hall, described in a colourful phrase by Vargas Llosa as 'un híbrido de restaurante-bar-dancing y burdel' (*28*, p.363); and an area of poor-quality housing rented out to people of precarious and limited means who live a world apart from the more prosperous citizens of the town.

In a substantial analysis of 'En este pueblo no hay ladrones', Vargas Llosa writes about the varied 'clase popular' of the town, which he summarises as 'la ralea: chulos, prostitutas, vagos, ladrones'; 'En el pueblo,' he elaborates, 'hay una rica vida, vulgar y vistosa, que ignorábamos' (*28*, pp.361–62). Vargas Llosa also makes the interesting claim that the perspective on the world that informs the narrative is that of the lower classes, including their views on matters such as love, justice and truth. This is a claim with which I shall take issue throughout the present chapter. Whereas there is no denying that the story follows closely the lives of a handful of characters lumped under Vargas Llosa's category of 'la ralea' and does indeed represent their points of view, it encompasses these within a broader narrative perspective and design attributable to the implied author, who fulfils a crucial role as editor and ultimate arbiter of the material. A relevant point of disagreement concerns the interpretation of the title, 'En este pueblo no hay ladrones'. For Vargas Llosa, the sentence expresses the triumph of social ideology, including common sense, over 'lo imaginario' and 'la sinrazón' personified in the story's central male protagonist, the layabout, ne'er-do-well and largely unthinking Dámaso (*28*, p.368). *Pace* the Peruvian novelist-critic, I maintain that the phrase is an act of critical ventriloquism and demystification of a community's self-image: over the course of its thirty-something pages, the narrative makes it abundantly clear that there *are* thieves in the town and that any claim to the contrary is misleading and self-deluding. Social ideology is certainly of paramount interest in 'En este pueblo no hay ladrones' (as it also is in the billiard saloon episode of 'La prodigiosa tarde de Baltazar' and elsewhere), but it emerges as something far more complex and questionable than allowed for in Vargas Llosa's reading of the story.

ii. The narrative

'En este pueblo no hay ladrones' sets itself apart from the stories examined so far by virtue of two features in particular, which are: the duration of the action (commensurate with the length of the narrative) and the complexity of relations between the numerous characters. The closest equivalent would be 'Un día después del sábado', where the narrative alternated between three characters (Sra. Rebeca, the old priest, and the young man from Manaure); but in that instance, the length of time covered by the story was under two days, which provided a unifying spatial and temporal frame for the diverse material of the narrative. The shortest time-span of all would be that of 'Un día de éstos' (two or three hours), followed by 'La siesta del martes' (close to four), but they are nothing compared with the duration of the action of 'En este pueblo no hay ladrones', which begins in June and concludes two months later on 'la noche del 20 de agosto' (pp.154–55). The coverage of that period is necessarily selective, with whole days, a week and, towards the end of the story, an entire fortnight being compressed into a single sentence, or completely elided.

The chronology of the story breaks down as follows: events begin early one Saturday morning in June with the robbery of three billiard balls from the local saloon and the culprit's return home to his pregnant wife; the shock waves of the robbery are charted through the remainder of the weekend and into Monday. There is then a leap forward to a subsequent (probably the following) Saturday and Sunday, with the action spilling over, as before, into the Monday morning. A physical break in the layout of the story occurs at this point, coinciding with the report of the forced embarkation onto a police launch, of a black man wrongly apprehended under suspicion of having committed the crime. A week goes by and the narrative advances to mid-July and, within a couple of pages, to the night of 20 August which, the showing of a film at the local cinema tells us, is another Saturday; the last substantial block of pages concentrate on the events of that night and extend into the early hours of Sunday, when the thief returns to the scene of his crime and is caught red-handed as he is about to replace the billiard balls in the box from which he had stolen them.

Apart from the uneven coverage of the passing of time, what is immediately noticeable about the story-line is the clustering of events around three weekends, with brief sections acting as 'padding' between the first and second, and the second and third weekends. This template accommodates events as follows: over the first weekend, the billiard balls are stolen and an innocent man apprehended. The following Sunday, the real culprit, Dámaso, goes to the local dance hall and spends the night with a prostitute, who is not distinguished by name. The third weekend, Dámaso re-visits the dance hall, gets drunk and this time assaults a male customer; he then returns home, collects the billiard balls and takes them to the billiard saloon, where he is caught by the owner, Don Roque. The narrative thus builds up to a dramatic climax on the final Saturday night and Sunday morning, when it involves Dámaso in a rash of events that seal his fate.

An alternative reading of the story is made possible through the insertion of a textual break between Dámaso's leaving the prostitute on the second Monday morning and the material that follows. Initially, the new paragraphs focus on Dámaso's wife, Ana, who is six months pregnant and feeling exhausted: 'se sentía agotada aquella mañana'. She nevertheless hurries to complete her collection of other people's dirty laundry so that she can go down to the river and witness 'el embarque del negro' (p.150) whom the police have been holding on suspicion of theft. At the jetty she encounters Dámaso. They converse, but neither of them says a word about where he has spent the night. The narrative then proceeds to concern itself with the black man, who has been abused by the police and is in a sorry state: 'Estaba sin camisa, el labio inferior partido y una ceja hinchada, como un boxeador'. In the following paragraph, the man has been tied to 'un tambor de petróleo' on board the police launch, which has left the jetty and is sailing away mid-stream. At exactly this moment, Ana utters an expression of sympathy ('— Pobre hombre — murmuró Ana'), which is echoed by a bystander, 'una mujer extraordinariamente gorda'. The episode then comes to a close with Ana walking Dámaso to the billiard saloon, where she leaves him, telling him to smarten up his appearance because, she says, he looks like 'un pordiosero' (p.151).

The episode is reminiscent, in its placing and effect, of the syntax of 'Un día después del sábado', where the narrative perspective shifted, late in the story, from the young man from Manaure to the priest and back again. The effect of the shift here is to privilege a female perspective on the inhuman treatment of the black man, shared between Ana and the woman standing by her. From the earlier point of the break in the text and for the duration of the time Ana spends with Dámaso, the narrative mobilises an alternative viewpoint from which to read the story being told: namely, from the viewpoint of a married woman, taken advantage of by her twenty-year-old husband who is seventeen years her junior, a layabout and petty criminal, amongst other things. Although Ana disappears, edited out of the narrative, for extended periods (for example, all the time that Dámaso spends in the dance hall and when he sets out to return the billiard balls to Don Roque's), she is no less important and compelling a subject of narrative interest, and the reader takes note of the need to complement his/her masculinist approach to the story with an approach that is woman-centred too.

iii. Secondary characters and sub-plots

Mention of the black man and of Don Roque points to the complexity of the narrative in terms of sub-plots and the relationships between the characters. As the 'fall guy' whom the police and others pick on and hold responsible for Dámaso's crime, the negro is his stand-in and partial double — not in the manner of the literary fantastic, analysed above with reference to the stories of *Ojos de perro azul* and the essay written by S. Meckled (*47*), but rather within the network of narrative relations that structure the story and form the basis of the social world depicted in it. A drifter and outsider, the negro finds himself in the wrong place at the wrong time and satisfies the local need for a scapegoat when a crime is committed. Even before he is apprehended, a week after the theft of the balls and in the cinema where a Cantinflas film is showing, one of the townsfolk has already insisted that the person responsible 'tuvo que ser [un forastero]', for the simple reason that 'En este pueblo no hay ladrones. Todo el mundo conoce a todo el mundo' (p.137). Between that statement and the black man's being apprehended, the police assume that they are looking for 'un forastero' and have already received reports of a sighting: 'Dicen que llegó el jueves y que anoche lo vieron dando vueltas por el puerto' (p.139). With the cards stacked so heavily against him, it can only be a matter of time before the drifter is caught and made to pay for Dámaso's crime. And even when a prostitute, Gloria, confirms that on the night of the theft he was with her and spent all the following day in her room, the authorities still refuse to release him; the mayor in fact threatens to imprison Gloria, 'por cómplice' (p.149), and stops intimidating her only after she has paid him the sum of twenty pesos. What the sub-plot involving the negro thus highlights, as much as the arbitrariness of fate, is the prevalence of injustice, cruelty and corruption in the town; the signal exceptions

to this norm are some of the women folk, who feel a sense of outrage and express sympathy for the negro in his hours of suffering (I provide further comment about the connection between the negro and Dámaso below).

The role of Don Roque in the narrative and the town is crucial. As the owner of the billiard hall where the men of the town go for recreation, he suffers a set-back when the balls are stolen and has to provide alternative activities for his customers. He must also make a declaration to the police about his financial loss, which he puts at two hundred pesos. As regards family and other relationships, he appears to be unmarried and welcomes the offer of assistance at the saloon from Dámaso, whom he addresses, colloquially, as 'hijo' (p.151). Don Roque is in fact old enough to be Dámaso's father, and there is a sense in which the younger man is seeking to come to terms, in the Oedipal scenario, with the principle of authority embodied in the father. At the end of the story, Don Roque enacts the Law of the Father on Dámaso, who remains paralysed when he is discovered trying to replace the three billiard balls. The Law of the Father proves to be an unjust law: by insisting that there were as many as two hundred pesos in the till on the night of the robbery, Don Roque, who knows that the real figure was much lower, cynically exploits the situation and will make Dámaso pay a disproportionate price for his crime. Smiling vindictively, he tells the young thief, 'Había doscientos pesos [...]. Y ahora te los van a sacar del pellejo, no tanto por ratero como por bruto' (p.164). This conclusion turns the tables on Dámaso, who finds himself in the galling position of the robber robbed. In the context of the town, it shows Don Roque to be no less corrupt than the mayor in his treatment of Gloria and the black drifter. Most pointedly of all, the conclusion reveals the emptiness and hypocrisy of the claim that there are no thieves in the town: Dámaso, Don Roque and the mayor all commit criminal acts which invalidate the self-image cultivated by the community and trumpeted in the claim, 'En este pueblo no hay ladrones'.

Another character who contributes to the complexity of narrative relations in the story is the young prostitute and single mother with whom Dámaso regularly spends the night. A secondary character like her would be out of place in most short stories, but not in 'En este pueblo no hay ladrones', which is considerably longer than average and home to a range of characters that appear as satellites of the main cast. The prostitute acts as a double of Ana, in much the same way that the negro stands in for Dámaso in the plot. Poignantly, she serves as a reminder of Ana's past, since, as we eventually learn, Ana too had spent many years entertaining men in her bedroom before marrying Dámaso (p.153). But the young prostitute also prefigures Ana's life as a mother beyond the temporal frame of the story. In that imaginary future, Ana will have to cope with a new-born child on her own, bereft of support and struggling to make ends meet; for all we know, she may have to fall back on prostitution as a means of survival. The 'aire desamparado' (p.150) of the young woman therefore reflects Ana's vulnerability with disturbing accuracy and relates to a wider spectrum of gender trouble which has Dámaso and Ana at its vortex.

iv. Gender trouble

> Sometimes it's hard to be a woman,
> Giving all your love to just one man.
> […] But if you love him, you'll forgive him
> Even though he's hard to understand.
> 'Stand by your man' (T. Wynette)

Twenty-first-century readers should be sensitized by now to the plight of the battered woman, highlighted in publications including Robin Norwood's blockbuster, *Women who Love Too Much*, and in countless reports of domestic violence that are carried on a virtually daily basis in the Western media. In Ana, García Márquez has created a female character who is long-suffering and stoical, and the personification of the virtues of patience and forgiveness popularised in 'Stand by your man' — the Country and Western classic taken to the top of the charts by Tammy Wynette in 1968. In Dámaso, the author has also mined popular culture and produced a two-dimensional figure combining aspects of Don Juan (or Jorge Negrete, in the story's American idiom) with the uneducated macho and machista who is easily provoked and dangerously insecure. In relation to a more canonical repertoire, García Márquez could also have drawn inspiration from stories by Chekhov such as 'The Huntsman', 'The Student', 'About Love', and 'At Christmas Time', all featuring women who are deprived of love, intimidated and, in the worst cases, beaten by their habitually drunken husbands. Grounded in a history of recurrent violence, the story of Ana and Dámaso is a cruel parody of a romance, held together by the woman's will, spirit of self-sacrifice, and what to the outsider seems inexplicable loyalty and love on her part.

The chemistry of Ana's relationship with her man is visible from the start when Dámaso returns home in the small hours of Saturday morning. A 'lámpara de petróleo [que] empezaba a extinguirse', fittingly casts a pall over Ana who has been waiting for hours, fully dressed and shod, for her husband to return. In the time he has been away she has had a nightmare, which she recounts thus: 'de pronto abrieron la puerta y te empujaron dentro del cuarto, bañado en sangre'. We gather from this that she is a woman of a nervous and a neurotic disposition. For his part, Dámaso comes across as surly and silent. Sensing from the start that he has caused concern through his absence, he attempts to pacify Ana with 'un gesto tranquilizador'. When that fails, he takes hold of her clumsily and 'con una violencia silenciosa' which she does not resist: 'Ana se dejó levantar casi en vilo. Luego descargó todo el peso del cuerpo hacia adelante, llorando contra la franela a rayas coloradas de su marido, y lo tuvo abrazado por los riñones hasta cuando logró dominar la crisis' (p.132). The incident is full of omens presaging physical violence and bodily harm. On the one hand, it shows what Dámaso is capable of doing, especially after he has been drinking. On the other, it conveys Ana's physical and emotional neediness, her passivity ('se dejó levantar') and susceptibility to horror — further emphasized by the graphic imagery of her nightmare.

The following days and weeks of the story show us an Ana who is stronger and more resourceful in her handling of Dámaso.

When he asks her to let him have a proportion of the rent money 'por pocos días', she resists, even though he grabs her forcefully by the wrist; all that day and night, she 'continuó inflexible' (p.146), intelligently anticipating his every move and not being fazed by his infantile threat to walk out and never return ever again. Indeed, the narrative disposes us to look on Ana favourably for the most part, admiring her patience, her sense of responsibility, and the sympathy that she feels for the black drifter, amongst other things. At the same time, we cannot overlook Ana's complicity in the cover-up of Dámaso's crime, but this is compensated for to an extent by the fact that she feels guilty, as does Dámaso, and eventually comes to the decision that he should return the balls to their rightful place in the saloon.

Recalling the earlier analysis of the narrative structure of 'En este pueblo no hay ladrones' and the way that it pivots around Ana's response to the embarkation of the negro on the second Monday morning of the story, we cannot help but notice the significant placing of two items of narrative material at that point. The first item centres, literally, on Ana's pregnant belly, which she invites Dámaso to feel when he returns from the billiard saloon, early on Tuesday morning. As reported, dead-pan, in the narrative,

> Dámaso no dio ninguna muestra de entusiasmo.
> — Ya está vivo — dijo Ana — . Se pasa la noche dándome pataditas por dentro.
> Pero él no reaccionó.

The absence of a reaction on Dámaso's part is perplexing: is he indifferent to Ana's condition? Or uncomfortable about it? Perhaps he intuits in her remarks the inevitability of a woman's fate, already internalised by Ana, to suffer physical violence, and the equal inevitability of that suffering being caused by the male from the time he is carried in his mother's womb (Ana refers to the foetus as masculine) until he reaches adulthood and full maturity. This hypothesis receives a measure of confirmation within the space of a few lines, when the narrative chooses to recall the very first instance of violence inflicted on Ana by Dámaso, near the beginning of their life together: 'Acaballado sobre ella en la cama, Dámaso la había golpeado hasta hacerla sangrar'. Compelling in its narrative directness, this item of material simply cannot be divorced from the earlier description of Ana inviting a reluctant Dámaso to put his hand on her belly and asking him, '¿No sientes?' (p.152). By placing the sensitive material so close to the break in the narrative which we interpreted earlier as a prompt to the reader to combine his/her masculinist approach with a woman-centred strategy of reading, García Márquez ensures that we pay due attention to Ana and experience fear and pity for her as prescribed in the Aristotelian theory of tragedy and its modern derivatives.

A peculiar feature, to say the least, of existing criticism of 'En este pueblo no hay ladrones' is the embarrassment obviously felt by a majority of male commentators at how, or even whether, they should address the episodes of wife-battering in the story. Vargas Llosa confronts the difficult material honestly and handles it by focusing on the wife-beater, Dámaso, whom he interprets as a stylized caricature of the 'macho prototípico' (*28*, p.364); Vargas Llosa is less interested in Ana's psychology, however. George McMurray makes no reference whatsoever to Dámaso's violent streak, in spite of the lengthy summary of the narrative that constitutes the bulk of his account of the story. Finally, Gene Bell-Villada expresses interest in the 'astoundingly primitive macho figure' cut by Dámaso (*8*, p.126) but then trivializes the story from any viewpoint that would take its subject, and Ana's suffering, seriously. Further points that are generally overlooked by critics are i) the awful inevitability of the final assault on Ana, a short while before Dámaso leaves the house for the billiard saloon, and ii) the discomfiting mixture of physical courage, strength of will and the attitude of self-sacrifice and abnegation that Ana displays when facing up to a drunken and senseless husband who is bent on returning the balls to Don Roque's saloon under circumstances that could not be more unpropitious.

The final assault committed by Dámaso on his wife now in the eighth month of pregnancy must be one of the most graphic and horrifying depictions of domestic violence in 'serious' literature. The assault takes place in the dead of night, in the confines of the couple's bedroom. Awakened by Dámaso's late and stumbling entry, Ana suddenly realises that he intends to go and break into the saloon and replace the balls there. She leaps out of bed and bars the door, saying earnestly, 'De aquí no sales mientras yo esté viva' (p.158). But Dámaso is in no mood to listen to reason and he tells her to step aside. When she will not, 'la agarró por el cabello, torció la muñeca y le hizo bajar la cabeza', in a movement which brings tears to her eyes. The violence escalates as Dámaso uses the bag containing the billiard balls to hit Ana around the knees, then the hands and finally lands a punch on her head, which sends her crashing into the wall and thence to the ground. The billiard balls assume their most hideous significance in this scene: a rather obvious symbol for the balls that Dámaso attributes to himself but in reality lacks, they are the tools, here, of male vindictiveness and victimization of the 'fairer sex', whose vulnerability is figured at its most pathetic in Ana's pregnant frame. At the start of the assault she warns Dámaso, 'Me vas a matar el muchacho en la barriga' (p.159), but he rides roughshod over her plea. Eventually losing all control, he shouts the ultimate insult, 'Puta' (p.160), which brings out his pent-up anger and probable contempt for women: all women, that is, regardless of whether they are mothers, wives or prostitutes, and pregnant or not. The element of misogyny and cowardice in Dámaso's psychological make-up is emphasized far too much to be excluded from considerations of his character.

Ana's behaviour in the climactic episode of the assault deserves separate comment. Her higher intelligence and moral awareness are obvious to the reader and stand in marked contrast to Dámaso's manifestly lower quotient of those attributes. With a mixture of admiration and concern, we note Ana's steely determination to prevent Dámaso from leaving the house and her desperation in hitting back at him when he has forced his way to the door. Especially interesting is her promise to take the balls back herself and thus to relieve Dámaso of the obligation to do so; because there is no guarantee that such an action will succeed, the offer demonstrates how far Ana might be willing to go to save the situation and, hopefully, the future of her relationship with Dámaso, on whom she feels dependent. Most significant of all from the point of view of the psychology of the battered wife is Ana's follow-up offer to sacrifice herself for Dámaso: she says, 'Puedo decir que fui yo [...]. Así como estoy, no pueden meterme en el cepo' (p.159). In the immediate narrative context, her words represent a last-ditch effort to prevent Dámaso from leaving the house. At a deeper level of personal psychology and gender politics, they bespeak an extreme attitude of abnegation and self-sacrifice on the part of a woman ready to 'stand by her man' whatever the consequences. Battered and bruised, Ana is a pointed example of the woman who loves too much and a worthy companion of literary antecedents such as Pelageya in Chekhov's 'The Huntsman', who, in spite of years of neglect at the hands of the unloving and drunk Yegor Vlasych, 'still watches his shoulder-blades moving, the raffish way his cap sits on the back of his head, his casual indolent stride, and her eyes fill with sadness and tender affection' (*60*, p. 6).

This focalized description of a Russian peasant coincides, perhaps unexpectedly, at various points with the image of a Colombian provincial conveyed in 'En este pueblo no hay ladrones': cocky, indolent, and the very picture of male narcissism. At an early stage in the narrative, García Márquez presents Dámaso in a humorous light that shades occasionally into ridicule — see, for example, the narrative's criticism of his ability to think up and immediately forget hare-brained schemes, so typical of the male in works by our author. Beneath this occasional light-heartedness, however, lies a deeply serious vein of concern about issues of masculinity, gender politics and the Law, which dominate the thematic structure of the story. The stolen billiard balls are an ever-present pointer to trouble affecting the society depicted in 'En este pueblo no hay ladrones'. It is hard to resist the jibe that Dámaso steals them because he lacks 'real balls'. This is most obvious in the final scene, where he is paralysed and effectively impotent in the presence of Don Roque. As the owner of the male-oriented saloon, he is custodian of the balls and appropriately has a name connoting rock-hardness. However, this is exposed as a pretense when Don Roque appears, in the final scene, 'sin lentes y sin la dentadura postiza' and looking like '[parecía] una mujer' (p.162). Márquez's critique here of the phallic order could not be more thorough-going or transparent.

Delving more deeply into the subject, we can appreciate more fully the incident that takes place earlier that same evening at the dance-hall between Dámaso and a salesman whom he assaults. The salesman is depicted as somewhat self-absorbed as he dances happily, first with two, and then with three women at once. We read that he 'era más pequeño que ellas' (p.156), and that Dámaso takes an instant dislike to him; eventually Dámaso cannot resist picking a fight and he punches the man in the face. The interpretation that the episode invites is that Dámaso feels affronted by a man more successful with the ladies than he feels himself to be. Dámaso, after all, enjoys favour with women and indeed lives off them. The little man from out of town therefore represents a challenge to his self-image but is really no contest.

The narrative of the evening's events highlights two further aspects of the gender trouble surrounding Dámaso. First, after the assault on the little man the narrative proceeds without a break to depict Dámaso refusing the offer of a spoonful of cooked rice from his companion, the anonymous prostitute at the dance-hall. He shakes his head, saying that 'Eso es para las mujeres [...]. Los machos no comemos' (p.157). Yet, his tone and body language, reminiscent of a bad-tempered child, are at odds with the pretentious rhetoric of machismo. The other matter of interest is the homosexual discourse of the cantinero, 'empolvado y con un clavel en la oreja' (p.147), who demands payment for the food and drink consumed by Dámaso and his woman friend. Dámaso reacts by pushing him to one side, saying 'No me gustan los maricas'. At this, the cantinero 'lo agarró por la manga', which shows that he is not afraid to mix it physically with someone his own size. Although they do not come to blows, the incident exposes the frailty of any claim that might assert an equivalence between conventionally-defined maleness and valour (the possession of balls), and gayness and the non-possession of that attribute. The episode pointedly leaves the last word to the cantinero, who replies to Dámaso's 'No me gustan los maricas': 'Pues no sabes lo que te pierdes' (p. 158). The astute placing of this material and all that surrounds it merely moments ahead of Dámaso's return home where he brutally assaults his wife, testifies to García Márquez's technical skill, especially the consummate art of suggestion which here disposes the reader to appreciate the complexity and range of gender trouble affecting Dámaso and the society around him.

v. Narrative art and sympathy in 'En este pueblo no hay ladrones'

An overarching assumption of the present Critical Guide is the realist cast of the majority of the narratives collected in *FMG*. Notwithstanding its abundance of symbolic motifs and archetypal resonances, a story such as 'La siesta del martes' demands to be read as exemplifying a realist aesthetic, comparable to the writing style of, say, Hemingway, which it imitates. In my reading of 'En este pueblo no hay ladrones', I have documented the fundamentally realistic handling of time and action and construed the characters as social and psychological types whose experiences of small-town life and gender politics, inter alia, are easily recognisable to most readers. I have also stressed the sympathy that the narrative evokes, through various means, for the black drifter and for Ana. An important point of reference and comparison in this respect is Chekhov, whose insightful and compassionate but generally unsentimental presentation of the dilemmas of female characters anticipates key aspects of both Hemingway and García Márquez's work. More will be said about the connection with Hemingway in the following chapter of this study. For present purposes, I wish to review some subtle and interesting mechanisms of narrative sympathy in 'En este pueblo no hay ladrones', drawing on the famous essay by Borges entitled 'El arte narrativo y la magia' (1932).

The subject of that essay is differing types of causality, disentangled from plot, that are available to writers of narrative fiction. Essentially, Borges distinguishes between, on the one hand, the 'concatenación de motivos' typical of most psychological novels, and, on the other, a 'primitiva claridad de la magia' that he associates with James George Frazer's 'law of sympathy' (*59*, p.230). Rejecting as unsuitable for the novel patterns of cause and effect which merely reflect real life, the Argentine writer prescribes 'un juego preciso de vigilancias, ecos y afinidades' (*59*, p. 231) which, he boldly claims, provide the only means of guaranteeing artistic integrity in a narrative. The clearest example of this procedure in Borges' own work might be 'Las ruinas circulares' from *Ficciones*, which belongs to the category of fantastic literature, as do many of the examples cited by Borges in 'El arte narrativo y la magia'. Without weakening the case for a predominantly realist reading of 'En este pueblo no hay ladrones', I suggest that the story also illustrates Borgesian 'laws of sympathy' operating at various levels of the text. A number of narrative and stylistic elements can be identified, which together constitute a rigorous scheme of 'vigilancias, ecos y afinidades' perceptible in the act(s) of reading.

These elements all refer to suffering, victimization and misfortune, starting with the black man, who, as we have seen, is beaten savagely by the police: 'Estaba sin camisa, el labio inferior partido y una ceja hinchada, como un boxeador' (p.151). The reader perhaps remembers the injuries sustained in the boxing ring by Carlos Centeno in 'La siesta del martes', where the dead son accrued pathos through the re-telling of his suffering. Some of that pathos rubs off onto the black man in 'En este pueblo no hay ladrones'. More remarkably, the boxing motif links the man to Dámaso, who is pictured twice weaving and skipping like a boxer: 'Dámaso ejecutó frente a [Ana] un pase de boxeo con la elasticidad de un profesional' (p.139), and 'Esa tarde, desde el lavadero, Ana lo vio llegar dando saltitos de boxeador' (p.144). Functioning in the first instance as an unexceptional detail of characterisation, the repeated motif eventually confirms Dámaso's ultimate responsibility, as the author of the robbery, for the black drifter's undeserved fate.

Imagery of blood and bleeding suffuses García Márquez's story, from start to finish. On the very first page, Ana recounts her nightmare of Dámaso's return to the house 'bañado en sangre' (p.132), which gives expression to her feelings of uneasiness and doom. Destined to evolve, in the course of García Márquez's oeuvre, into Plácida Linero's troubled dream at the beginning of *Crónica de una muerte anunciada* (1981), Ana's foreboding sets the scene for three later, related incidents. The first of these is the violent capture of the negro at the cinema, where he receives blows to the face that leave him 'con la cara embadurnada de un amasijo de polvo, sudor y sangre' (p.141). The second involves a metaphorical use of the verb 'desangrarse', applied to the town late one night when a dispirited and aimless Dámaso leaves the billiard saloon and 'se encontró sin rumbo en una plaza que parecía desangrarse' (p.147); in Dámaso's view, it is as if the very life-blood of the town is haemorrhaging away. Finally, the scene of Ana's first abuse at Dámaso's hands bears witness to the fact that he drew blood, punching her 'hasta hacerla sangrar' (p.152). Together, these references build up a cumulative pattern which establishes a spiritual and aesthetic affinity between Ana, the black man and a town that is emptying of signs of life.

Ana's suffering is displaced onto two other, apparently unrelated objects. The first of these is the set of billiard balls, which we have interpreted above as symbolising the phallic order. That interpretation still stands, but it needs to be nuanced in order to take account of associations that are conveyed the first time the balls are mentioned. Struggling to control her nerves and with the package containing the balls nestling in her lap, Ana 'soltó los nudos y vio: eran tres bolas de billar, dos blancas y una roja, sin brillo, estropeadas por los golpes' (pp.132–33). The image anticipates our later discovery of Ana's history of assault and battery. We shall read about how a life of hardship has left her feeling 'estropeada' at the age of thirty seven: comparing herself with her more youthful and handsome husband, whose eyes are an irresistible attraction not only to women but also to the gay 'cantinero' (p.147), she sees herself as 'madura y desarreglada' (p.139). The fact that the balls are in some sense a metonymy of the billiard saloon where male society congregates in the town, only reinforces the message that Ana, a former prostitute, has been worn out and beaten into virtual submission by the patriarchal system.

The other object that is 'sympathetic' to Ana is the door through which Dámaso gains entry into Don Roque's billiard hall. Referred to at the first mention as 'la puerta violada' (p. 137), it retains that somewhat melodramatic epithet right through to the final episode when Dámaso returns to the scene of his crime and effects entry through the same doorway: 'Esta vez no tuvo que servirse de la linterna. La puerta sólo había sido reforzada en el sitio de la orgolla violada' (pp.160–61). Through the emotive word 'violada', the door comes to embody the sexually- or, more precisely, the gender-motivated violence that has been visited on Ana in the past and that she will suffer again before the story is over. Complementing the motifs of boxing, blood and balls surveyed here, the motif of violation spills over from one level of the narrative onto another, in a striking display of Borgesian 'sympathy' between character, setting and action.

The atmosphere of suffering and misfortune that hangs over 'En este pueblo no hay ladrones' merges subtly with that of three other contemporary works by García Márquez, in a manner that is redolent, again, of Borges' work. The description of the damaged door at Don Roque's saloon includes a detail that refers back to an earlier story in the volume, which is 'Un día de éstos': the sentence, 'El candado estaba intacto, pero una de las argollas había sido arrancada como una muela' (p.137), reprises the image of the mayor's rotten tooth and repeats the agony associated with its extraction. At a later stage in 'En este pueblo no hay ladrones', Ana cannot possibly know the intratextual reverberations of her assessment of the fruitless robbery committed by her husband, but the reader picks them out instantly: ' — La mala hora –dijo Ana' (p.153), citing the title phrase of the novella on which García Márquez was already at work at the time. Less substantial, perhaps, is the echo of the colonel's situation in *El coronel no tiene quien le escriba*, which informs the description of women in the dance-hall visited by Dámaso: 'juiciosamente sentadas contra la pared, parecían a la espera de una carta' (p.156). Examples, not so much of the Frazer- and Borges-derived principle of 'sympathy' as of the transgression of boundaries between discreet works of imaginative literature, the instances recorded here bear witness to a possibly ludic dimension of intertextuality in the stories of *FMG*.

There remains one final motif to account for in the narrative fabric of 'En este pueblo no hay ladrones': I refer to the enormous white cat that Dámaso tells Ana he encountered when he broke into the billiard hall, at the beginning of the story. Mario Vargas Llosa has written at length about the cat, which he regards as a cipher of mystery belonging to the same category as the two hundred pesos that Don Roque alleges were stolen in the break-in. According to Vargas Llosa, the two hundred pesos may never have existed in (the story's) reality but they are surrounded by sufficient ambiguity to make it impossible for us to dismiss them as a complete fabrication. Along with the money, the cat is important to Vargas Llosa because it fits the category of 'lo imaginario' that he insists informs all of García Márquez's fictions to a lesser or greater degree. As he proceeds with his analysis of works up to and including *Cien años de soledad*, Vargas Llosa looks for 'datos escondidos elípticos' (*28*, p. 369) which will support his thesis that the works combine 'lo real objetivo' with subjective constructions ('lo imaginario') that qualify and eventually cancel out the objective pretensions of the narrative. In the case of 'En este pueblo no hay ladrones', the Peruvian author-critic's essentially phenomenological approach arguably works better with the two hundred pesos than with the cat, and can usefully be complemented by an approach that reflects the story's concerns with issues of psychology and gender.

The cat appears twice in the course of García Márquez's narrative. It does so first when Dámaso recounts his experiences inside the billiard hall, on his return home. As he explains to Ana,

— Había un gato allá adentro — dijo — . Un enorme gato blanco.
— ¿Estabas muy asustado?
— ¿Yo?

— Tú—dijo Ana — . Dicen que los hombres también
se asustan.

El la sintió sonreír, y sonrió.

— Un poco — dijo — . No podía aguantar las ganas de
orinar. (p.134)

The exchange establishes a clear link between the cat, the spectre of
fear, and a perceived threat to manhood. Speaking with unusual
frankness, Dámaso admits to having felt fear in the presence of the
cat, just like any other man or woman caught off guard; what is
more, he locates the physical symptom of fear in the lower
abdomen, which reinforces the intimation of vulnerability. A couple
of pages later, the tell-tale description of Dámaso's 'diáfanos ojos de
gato' (p.136) identifies him pointedly with the very animal that
instilled fear in him, and suggests a complex psychological
dimension to the incident of his encounter with the cat.

The animal reappears near the end of the narrative when
Dámaso returns to the billiard hall on the doomed second leg of his
mission. Surrounded by a ghostly aura, it would seem to originate in
Dámaso's psyche as much as in objective circumstance:

… Allí estaba el gato.

El animal lo miró sin misterio a través de la luz.
Dámaso lo siguió enfocando hasta que recordó con un
ligero escalofrío que nunca la había visto en el salón
durante el día. Movió la linterna hacia adelante,
diciendo: 'Zape', pero el animal permaneció impasible.
Entonces hubo una especie de detonación silenciosa
dentro de su cabeza y el gato desapareció por completo
de su memoria. Cuando comprendió lo que estaba
pasando, ya había soltado la linterna y apretaba el
paquete de las bolas contra el pecho. El salón estaba
iluminado. (pp.161–62)

The narrative is ambiguous about the cat's 'real', objective existence, which initially it asserts but then deliberately calls into question by suggesting that the animal is an effect of Dámaso's memory and an accident of perception. The realisation by Dámaso that he had never seen the cat in the billiard hall during daytime unsettles his nerves and opens up the possibility that the cat is a fantastic apparition. That hypothesis credits the animal with a certain presence, which would be in line with Vargas Llosa's phenomenological approach to the place of the animal in the narrative. However, it is equally possible to view the cat as a projection of Dámaso's mind and therefore as a purely psychic phenomenon. This interpretation mirrors the narrative emphasis on mental activity and memory, also accommodating the important detail of the face-to-face between Dámaso and the cat. In the billiard hall, Dámaso comes face to face with a gaze against which he is, for once, powerless. Linked to his impotence in the presence of Don Roque, the gaze of the cat would seem to give expression to fear and guilt that Dámaso cannot control and that pull him inexorably towards his fate. Certainly, the cat exemplifies the category of 'lo real imaginario' that abounds in Márquez's fiction, but in the narrative context of 'En este pueblo no hay ladrones' it derives its primary rationale from the male character's psychology, which is depicted in unusually vivid and compelling terms.

vi. Conclusion

The critical fortunes of 'En este pueblo no hay ladrones' have been mixed, with a number of commentators disputing the story's artistic merit. For one critic, 'the story's artistic merit and dramatic appeal are greatly reduced by its excessive length. Indeed, because entire episodes add little or nothing to the central theme, this is one of the least successful pieces of the collection' (20, p.52). In the light of the analysis conducted in this chapter, it is difficult to accept such an evaluation of 'En este pueblo no hay ladrones'. The story stands out as one of the most coherent in the collection, especially when read from the perspectives of gender and psychology that I have emphasized here. A focus on the 'dull, backwater existence' of the town and the ironies that result from human weaknesses (*20*, p.52) is a valid reflection, perhaps, on Dámaso's character and circumstances, but it fails to tell us anything about the deep-seated motivations of his relationships with other people ranging from Ana, through the bartender and the little man whom he assaults in the dance-hall, to don Roque. In terms of narrative artistry, 'En este pueblo no hay ladrones' is also more complex than commentators such as McMurray and Bell-Villada have allowed. The concept of 'sympathy' is a useful tool for gaining access to the mechanisms of this story, which chime in with those analysed in previous chapters and foreshadow those to come.

5. 'Rosas artificiales' and 'La viuda de Montiel': Women without Men

The sub-title of this chapter evokes a famous collection of stories by Hemingway called 'Men without Women' and reverses the constituent terms in order to emphasize the emerging prominence of female concerns in the stories of *FMG*. The abused figure of Ana in 'En este pueblo no hay ladrones', though neglected by a majority of the critics and not quite in the same moral league as Carlos Centeno's faultless mother in 'La siesta del martes', clearly illustrates García Márquez's sensitivity to women and woman-related issues, and paves the way for the concentration of and on women in the sixth and seventh stories of the collection. The fictional worlds of 'Rosas artificiales' and 'La viuda de Montiel' are noteworthy, in particular, for the absence of men folk, which is total in the first case and almost so in the second. This circumstance is explicable in the case of Montiel's widow through the event of the eponymous husband's death; in 'Rosas artificiales', matters are more complex and intriguing because the men folk who might have any conceivable relation to the domestic setting are effectively edited out, condemned to a shadowy existence like the denizens of the world that lies off-stage and outside Bernarda Alba's house in the famous play by Federico García Lorca. The concentration on women's affairs in 'Rosas artificiales' and 'La viuda de Montiel' endows both narratives with a density of texture and an allusiveness that make them outstanding examples of the poetic possibilities of the short story form.

'*Rosas artificiales*'

i. The narrative

After 'Un día de éstos', 'Rosas artificiales' is the shortest of the stories in *FMG*, followed closely by 'La viuda de Montiel' and 'La siesta del martes'. With 'Un día de éstos' it shares a temporal frame of reference and duration starting at daybreak and lasting through mid-morning until roughly midday. However, the fact that 'Rosas artificiales' occupies exactly double the number of pages and lines of print as 'Un día de éstos', results in an appreciable difference in the pace and density of the narrative, which is deliberately sparse in events and attentive, instead, to the emotional vicissitudes of the main character. Although the narrative gives no details of Mina's age, we can imagine her to be a young woman, probably in her twenties and certainly nubile; for a living, Mina makes artificial flowers in what the narrative rather grandly calls her 'taller' or workshop, set up each morning in the main room of the house that she shares with her mother and her grandmother. Mina's relationship with the latter, who is blind, is close enough for the two women to share the same bedroom; the narrative also evidences the strength of Mina's emotional bond with her grandmother, who, in the course of the story, will display uncanny insight into her granddaughter's understated but turbulent emotional life. Mina, in turn, will unload a range of feelings including anger and frustration onto her grandmother, who thus becomes the target of emotions displaced from their primary site.

The structure of 'Rosas artificiales' repeats the tripartite format encountered in earlier stories such as 'Un día de éstos' and 'En este pueblo no hay ladrones' (when read as centering around Dámaso). Section one features Mina and the grandmother and covers the first couple of hours of daylight on a Friday morning that we are told expressly is the first of the month. There are some weeks to go before Easter, and Mina is looking for the long sleeves ('mangas') that she must wear if she is to be allowed to attend mass celebrated by the parish priest, father Angel. The grandmother informs her that she washed the sleeves the previous night, and this draws a curt response from Mina, who snaps, 'No vuelvas a coger mis cosas' (p.209). The grandmother follows up with a second remark that is intended to be helpful: she advises Mina to put a piece of paper underneath the sleeves in order to prevent contact with the grimy stone surface on which they are drying. Mina, however, dismisses this practical suggestion and retorts, 'Si se ensucian tú eres la responsable'. With time running out, Mina puts on the sleeves although they are still damp, she removes some make-up ('colorete') that she had worn the previous night and leaves the house, only to return fifteen minutes later claiming that she could not attend mass because she is improperly dressed. She now subjects the grandmother to a double salvo of complaint, telling her, 'Tú tienes la culpa' (p.210) and 'Tienes que confesarte, porque me hiciste perder la comunión del primer viernes'. The reader cannot help feeling that Mina is being unfair to the grandmother and reacting with a vehemence that is disproportionate to the situation, whatever that may be. Why all the fuss about the sleeves and being properly dressed for mass, we ask ourselves, if Mina in the end stays away? What has happened in the quarter of an hour that has elapsed between her leaving the house and then returning in such a tearful state? The situation outlined up to this point may be more complex than is apparent at first sight. The possibility that Mina might be implicated in some kind of moral drama occurs to Mina's grandmother, and she relays this idea to the reader via the self-justificatory remark, 'Dios sabe que tengo la conciencia tranquila' (p.211), uttered as Mina withdraws into the privacy of the bedroom.

Mina's departure coincides with the first-time entrance of her mother, who asks the grandmother, '¿Con quién hablas?' as she enters the room. The grandmother's answer is in keeping with the atmosphere of secrecy and obliqueness that pervades the narrative: 'Con nadie — dijo la ciega — . Ya te he dicho que me estoy volviendo loca' (p.211). Since there has been no prior evidence of mental instability on the grandmother's part, the reader assumes that this is a semi-comic remark designed to keep Mina's mother in the dark about the whole business of the sleeves, the mass and

Mina's affective state. A cut to the bedroom immediately thickens
the air of mystery. The narrative shows Mina opening a box that she
keeps under lock and key inside the wardrobe; from it she takes out
a packet of letters that are tied with an elastic band and then returns
the box to its hiding place. Concealing the letters in the folds of her
underwear, she goes to the bathroom and throws them down the
lavatory pan, without any clarification being supplied for the benefit
of the reader. A narrative cut back to Mina's mother and
grandmother reinforces the impression of the mother's exclusion
from the circuit of information relating to her daughter. Intercepting
a remark directed at Mina, the grandmother volunteers a plausible
explanation for her not being at mass, and Mina and she together
collude in the pretence that she could not attend because she has
been busy producing large quantities of roses commissioned by
father Angel for Holy Week. Invisible to the mother, the complicity
between grandmother and granddaughter at this point in the story is
plain for the reader to see.

Taking stock of the first section of 'Rosas artificiales', we
understand the story to be about female emotions, mores and family
relationships in a small town where women such as Mina are
constrained by codes of gender, morality and religion. We sense, as
the grandmother does, a tension in Mina's mood and life, rooted in
concerns about sexual propriety — we note the persistent mention of
the 'mangas postizas' and the passing reference to the rouge that
Mina must remove before setting off for church — and a probable
romance, signalled by the collection of letters which we assume
document a history of intimacy between Mina and an unidentified
partner. In respect of family relationships, the story depicts different
degrees of closeness between three generations of women in Mina's
family and establishes a framework of dramatic irony around the
relation of complicity that exists between two of the women and the
effective marginalisation of the third member of the triad.

Section two of the story begins before seven o'clock and
encapsulates a period of three hours in which Mina is joined by her
co-worker and confidante, Trinidad. When Trinidad leaves the
house 'antes de las diez' (p.213), the precise temporal markers help

to create a realistic sense of time's passing and of the rhythms of a
working day. The action of this segment of the narrative centres on
the production of roses made out of 'papel elástico' (p.212) and
other paraphernalia that are handled expertly by Trinidad and Mina.
Just before the half-way point of the segment and of the story,
attention shifts abruptly from the roses to a shoe-box that Trinidad
has brought to the house with her and which she says contains, of
all things, dead mice! This is a statement which will be shown,
within the space of a page, to be true and which readers familiar
with García Márquez's novella, La mala hora, will be able to match
to its fictional world where Trinidad helps keep the church clean by
setting traps for mice and collecting up the dead bodies for disposal,
in a shoe-box. Not necessarily privy to that knowledge, the reader of
'Rosas artificiales' experiences a jolt at the first mention of the
mice, which creates effects of surprise and dissonance that are a
recurrent feature of García Márquez's writing style.

After the 'golpe' of the shoe-box, the narrative concentrates
once more on the central activity of women making flowers 'en la
sala decorada con cuadros idílicos y fotografías familiares'. These
details of domestic décor call attention to issues of happiness and
family unity in Mina's home and create a mood that is at once cosy
and out of place. A cameo of Trinidad working 'con admirable
pulcritud, moviendo apenas los dedos, las piernas muy juntas',
depicts a young woman who is delicate, domesticated and prim.
That impression is immediately strengthened by the narrative's
registering Trinidad's embarrassment when she notices Mina
looking at her 'zapatos masculinos': the fleeting description of
Trinidad 'apenas arrastrando los pies hacia atrás' (p.212) is a
brilliant illustration of a writer's intuition and skill in finding the
perfect dramatic vehicle for expressing subtle shades of feeling.
At this finely poised moment of (in-)delicacy, the narrative
includes a brief but significant exchange between Mina and
Trinidad. The exchange, comprising three questions of one or two
words and three answers of two or three, refers to an unnamed
individual who Mina confirms has left town. We assume that the
individual is a man and that his departure was unexpected.

According to the narrative, the conversation allows Mina to unburden herself of '[el] peso de su intimidad', but the reader is provided with no hard information about Mina's relationship, the nature of her feelings, or the full implications of the man's departure. The last question asked by Trinidad, '¿Y ahora?', elicits the response, 'Ahora, nada', which Mina articulates 'sin temblor en la voz' (p.213). On that non-committal note, the exchange ends and Trinidad takes her leave.

Clearly, the exchange and all that surrounds it is crucial to the story of Mina and her life. We immediately sense the painful relevance to her situation of the 'cuadros idílicos y fotografías familiares' (p.212) found in the main room, and infer that she has been abandoned by a lover. The subtle emphasis on Trinidad's body-language and inappropriate shoes raises issues of gender and sex which are not clarified by the action that closes this edgy and suggestive segment of the narrative: 'Liberada del peso de su intimidad, Mina la retuvo [a Trinidad] un momento, para echar los ratones muertos en el excusado'. Indeed, creating and maintaining a sense of strangeness and mystery seems to be a deliberate stratagem on the author's part, since it carries over quite conspicuously into the opening lines of the following section, which brings the grandmother back into the frame. As she moves through the patio to dispose of the mice, Mina passes her grandmother and comments, 'A que no sabes qué llevo en esta caja'. The conundrum is not difficult for the reader to solve, but for the grandmother it poses a real problem, since she is blind. Taunting her rather cruelly, Mina gives her a clue, but only an auditory one: she shakes the box ('Hizo sonar los ratones') as many as three times. The grandmother nevertheless fails to produce the solution to the conundrum and Mina informs her, somewhat triumphantly, 'Son los ratones que cayeron anoche en las trampas de la iglesia' (p. 213). The incident is important for many reasons. In rhetorical terms, it makes the reader feel privileged about being 'in the know', but also uncomfortable about the grandmother's sensorial deprivation. At the same time, we should recognise that the blind woman's struggle to comprehend is a mirror image of our own attitude to the text,

which contains elements of mystery and incompleteness that amount
to a puzzle.

In truth, the grandmother is overall less 'in the dark' than any
of us. An earlier reference to her 'mirada clarividente' (p.210) and
her intuitive grasp of the slightest change in Mina's mood had
signalled possession of extraordinary insight and a sure ability,
notwithstanding her blindness, to 'read' a situation as it unfolded
around her. That ability is put on display throughout the final
section of the story, which comprises a lengthy passage of dialogue
between the grandmother and Mina and brings the story full circle.
After Trinidad's departure, Mina wants to finish off the morning's
work and, presumably, to take stock of events. She surrounds herself
with a private wall of silence, which the grandmother breaches,
saying, 'Mina. Si quieres ser feliz, no te confieses con extraños'
(p.213). This statement sets Mina aback, because it assumes, quite
correctly, that she has confided in Trinidad. She utters no response,
however. A further statement by the grandmother is more difficult
for her to ignore, because it reconstructs the morning's events with
uncanny and uncomfortable accuracy. Demolishing Mina's earlier
pretence that she had been crying because she had missed the early
morning mass, the grandmother alleges that she had gone out of the
house on another, less innocent mission and that 'En el camino te
esperaba alguien que te ocasionó una contrariedad'. That this is true
is confirmed by Mina's passing her hands 'frente a los ojos de la
abuela' and admitting, 'Eres adivina' (p.214). And, when the
grandmother proceeds with unerring logic to dissect Mina's other
actions including her retrieval of the letters from the wardrobe and
the unusual event of her going to the lavatory twice that morning
instead of just once as is her norm, Mina knows that she has been
'rumbled' by one who, apart from being gifted with extraordinary
insight, also possesses vastly superior dialectical powers.

It is ironic that the person who saves Mina from final
embarrassment should be her mother, who, entering from the
corridor, asks casually, '¿Qué es lo que pasa?', and thereby
unwittingly puts a stop to her own mother's discomfiture of Mina.
Her unsuspecting question has ramifications of which she cannot be

aware: on a metaliterary level, the question could apply to the story
that we are reading, which even now is difficult to summarise for
the benefit of an outsider or latecomer; on a more immediate
dramatic level, it provides the grandmother with an opportunity to
expose Mina and the story of her secret love. However, given what
has gone before, it would be wholly inconsistent for the
grandmother to betray Mina, and indeed she does not. Honouring
the ties of closeness and understanding that bind them together, she
deflects attention away from Mina's predicament and, in answer to
her own daughter's question, says, 'Que estoy loca [...]. Pero por lo
visto no piensan mandarme para el manicomio mientras no empiece
a tirar piedras' (p.215). This boutade elaborates on her earlier
remark, 'Ya te he dicho que me estoy volviendo loca' (p.211), and
formally brings the narrative full circle. In respect of family
relationships, it reinforces the mother's exclusion from the tightly-
knit order inhabited by the grandmother and Mina, who have
occupied centre stage for most of the story. Of the three characters,
the mother is the one who emerges with least credit, leaving us with
the impression that she has little or no idea about what is happening
in her own home, let alone in the world outside. The grandmother
comes across as strong, clever and full of insight into the lives of
women. And Mina projects sadness and frustration at being
abandoned by her lover — emotions that she plays out in the bad-
tempered conversations she has with her grandmother and in the
manual production of the 'rosas artificiales' of the story's title.

ii. Artifice and artistry

The above analysis of narrative structure, tone and plot in 'Rosas
artificiales' supports the claim made by Bell-Villada that the story
'has unusual art and subtlety even for García Márquez' (8, pp.121–
22). I have drawn attention to qualities of strangeness and mystery,
dissonance and irony which inform the story and derive from the
way it is told. The raw material out of which 'Rosas artificiales' is
hewn is a body of emotions which, in the case of Mina, are deep and
complex and rendered accessible to the reader through mechanisms
of deflection and displacement. I have also hinted at a meta-literary

dimension in 'Rosas artificiales', which opens with a description of Mina 'moviéndose a tientas en la penumbra del amanecer' (p.209), groping for a fixed point of reference in half-light that adumbrates the hermeneutic difficulties that the text will present to the reader. In this connection, the blindness that afflicts the grandmother is a telling metaphor of incomprehension (being 'in the dark'), the effects of which the grandmother herself is spared through a pointed irony that works, rather unkindly, against her fully-sighted but basically clueless daughter. There may be an implied message for the reader in all this.

As in 'En este pueblo no hay ladrones', some of the mechanisms for engaging the reader in 'Rosas artificiales' suggest a link with Borges, and that is a connection that can be pursued through a numerical motif that calls to mind the canonical story, 'La muerte y la brújula'. The reader will remember how, in that story from *Ficciones*, Erik Lönnrot investigates a series of murders that seem to respond to a logic based on the Tetragrammaton and the four cardinal points. Unfortunately for Lönnrot, he makes a mistaken assumption about the last assassination in the series and ends up dead, trapped in a web of numbers and cunning that has been spun by the assassin. In 'Rosas artificiales' the number that sheds light on the business of interpretation is 3. We have noted the structural division of the story into three sections and its cast of three women, each from a different generation. As we shall see shortly, the narrative also gives prominence to three objects that are rich in symbolic meaning: they are Mina's sleeves, the letters she throws down the lavatory pan, and the artificial roses that she makes with Trinidad. The motif of throwing something down the lavatory is mentioned three times. A number of secondary details further confirm the importance of 3 over other numbers such as 1 or 2: when Mina leaves the house, ostensibly to attend mass, it is after she hears the 'tercer toque' of the church bells (p.210). The keys that hang around Mina's neck and that she uses to unlock her stash of love letters number three, as we read in the second and third sections of the narrative. And, the grandmother has three goes at solving the conundrum of the shoe-box.

The crop of patterns of three in the story's design throws light on a detail of the narrative which might not otherwise register with us: this is the elliptically told story of Mina's abandonment. On its own, abandonment by her lover causes Mina profound sorrow and awakens the sympathy of Trinidad and, by extension, the reader. Set against the background of past and present relationships in the family, it extends a sad history of female abandonment by men: on the evidence made available in the text, neither the grandmother nor the mother has enjoyed a lasting relationship with a husband or partner who could be a father-figure to their respective daughters. And that raises the question, is Mina condemned to the same fate? Furthermore, and most critically of all, is she pregnant? The ternary logic of the story dictates this outcome and suggests that she faces a life identical to those of her forebears: a life without a man who might care for her and behave responsibly towards the child she may already have conceived. Accordingly, Mina stands to fare no better than Ana in 'En este pueblo no hay ladrones' or the mother of Carlos Centeno and his surviving sister in 'La siesta del martes', or her own mother and grandmother in 'Rosas artificiales'. The proposition that Mina is pregnant is not articulated expressly, but it is certainly implied in Trinidad's final question, '¿Y ahora?' (p.213). In my experience teaching this story, I have found that women readers in particular respond sympathetically to the suggestion that Mina is pregnant and indeed have often volunteered that hypothesis spontaneously in discussion. Dealing with a text that is so visibly contrived and elliptical and buzzing with that 'palpitación de vida' that García Márquez valorized in his aesthetic creed, there is every justification for accepting the hypothesis of Mina's pregnancy and incorporating it into our interpretation.

Playing with numbers is not, of course, exclusive to the work of Jorge Luis Borges, nor is it the only motif that thickens the narrative texture of 'Rosas artificiales'. Borges is also just one among many influences and intertexts that are embedded in García Márquez's story, which arguably stands in a closer relationship to Chekhov and Hemingway than to the Argentinian master. Aside from García Márquez's frank hero-worship of Hemingway, documented in an earlier chapter of this Guide, a handful of critics have linked specific stories, including 'La mujer que llegaba a las seis' and 'La siesta del martes', to Hemingway (*42*, p.61), whilst several others have asserted a wider-ranging and more pervasive influence of Hemingway on García Márquez (*23*). Key ingredients of the recipe shared between the two authors are: the iceberg principle, realism, and a repertoire of narrative and stylistic procedures that invest writing in prose with powers of suggestion more usually ascribed to poetry. 'Rosas artificiales' provides compelling evidence of García Márquez's assimilation of Hemingway in all these respects.

Arguably, there is no more economical and accomplished translation of Hemingway's iceberg theory than the obliquely-told and elliptical story of Mina's love affair. We recall that the theme surfaces, very briefly, in the conversation that Mina holds with Trinidad just after the half-way point of 'Rosas artificiales'. As tips of icebergs go, the six lines of parsimonious dialogue, interwoven with five lines of absolutely neutral narrative, are slight but pregnant with a weight of meaning that the reader can only intuit first time round; the amount of matter that lies below the surface of the narrative is huge and will only become visible through close and repeated scrutiny. The Hemingway corpus includes a thematic and technical counterpart in 'Hills like White Elephants', where an American couple waiting at a railway station in north-eastern Spain skirt around the topic of 'an awfully simple operation' that the woman seems willing to undergo, for the sake of the marriage. The husband's reassurance that it is 'not really an operation at all' (*67*, p.275) is belied by an undercurrent of mounting tension and by the wife's eventual request to him to 'please please please please please please please stop talking' (*67*, p. 277). What is never spelt out is the exact nature of the operation that promises to restore the couple's love and happiness. The reader assumes that the wife must undergo a gynaecological procedure and that the couple's relationship is sexually dysfunctional, but the narrative provides no hard information to confirm this supposition, and we are left clutching at straws.

The title of Hemingway's story comments obliquely on the human drama that is contained within its short form. 'Hills like White Elephants' picks up on a phrase that the wife uses to describe the landscape of Spain's Ebro region in a season when 'the country was brown and dry' (67, p.273). There is an implication of sterility in the quotation, but it only becomes clear in retrospect and then, perhaps, only to the reader who is attuned to Hemingway's finely allusive style. A comparison with García Márquez's practice in 'Rosas artificiales' is instructive, because he provides even less narrative information about Mina's predicament than Hemingway does in his treatment of the couple's troubled intimacy in 'Hills like White Elephants'. Additional comparisons with stories such as 'The Sea Change' or 'A Canary for One', would reinforce the conclusion that, by the time he wrote 'Rosas artificiales', García Márquez had become a master-practitioner of the allusive power inherent in the theory of the iceberg.

Hemingway's 'realism' is an essential part of his narrative art and an example which also shines through in 'Rosas artificiales'. In the fashioning of terse dialogue, the expression of his characters' psychology, the rendering of the passage of time, and in his adherence to linear structure, García Márquez aligns himself quite clearly with Hemingway's favoured procedures of composition and his skilful representation of the real. By way of an example, the story 'Cat in the Rain' works the artistic miracle of intimating the understated drama that lies at the heart of a young wife's empty life. Looking out of the window of a hotel in Italy where she is staying with her husband, the woman — an American — sees a cat sheltering from a shower of rain and insists that she must bring it inside and care for it. She goes out into the rain to fetch the cat, but, by the time she reaches the place where she saw it sheltering, it has disappeared. Her admission that 'I don't know why I wanted it so much' (67, p.169), testifies to her underlying ignorance of the strong feelings that move her. A subsequent outburst, redolent of a spoilt child, hints at the emptiness of her married life and the probable role of the cat as a substitute for the child that the couple do not have. For the full duration of the story, the woman's husband, George, sits propped up in bed reading and showing no obvious inclination to start a family. When the hotelier sends up the maid with the cat, we sense that the wife will feel relief and even temporary fulfilment, but the story has exposed the emotional and sexual void at the centre of her life and augurs badly for the future.

Compared with 'Cat in the Rain', 'Rosas artificiales' depicts a situation of equal, if not greater drama in a young woman's life. The emotional undercurrents are somewhat different, and the circumstances of the two women, diametrically opposed: whereas the young woman longs for a child to bring happiness to her marriage, Mina faces the probable prospect of bringing up an illegitimate child without the help of a husband. In spite of these differences, each story is a model of realism, in its own terms. Mina's story, in particular, mirrors the sociological realities of male sexual irresponsibility and fractured family life in a society where the Catholic Church endeavours to control its female members, does what it can to promote domestic harmony, and has only limited success in these ventures. On the basis of the story's objective treatment of the themes of guilt, non-communication and loneliness, and their presentation 'in precise, linear form', George McMurray evaluated 'Rosas artificiales' as one of its author's 'most realistic pieces of short fiction' (20, p.51).

A final aspect, and veritable hallmark of the literary artistry of García Márquez and Hemingway is the symbolism they weave into the fabric of their narratives. The symbols refer to climate, landscape and countless natural and man-made objects, and serve to enrich various components of the stories, including character, situation and event, and the creation of a mood or prevailing atmosphere; as happens with the brown and barren landscape in 'Hills like White Elephants', the symbols typically cast light or shadow onto the dramas affecting the characters and thereby enhance the emotional and thematic texture of the plot. A frequent type of symbolic motif in Hemingway's work makes a pointed comment, from a position of apparent inconsequentiality, on the main issue of human interest. This is the case of the horse on which the bartender has placed a bet in 'The Sea Change': all the time his

mind is on the race, a male customer argues with his girlfriend in
the bar and fails to prevent her from walking out on him, not for
another man but for a woman. The outcome of this particular 'two-
horse race' leaves the customer angry and disconsolate, and he
confides to the bar-tender, 'I'm a different man, James [...].You see
in me quite a different man' (*67*, p.401).

We have documented the presence and function of various
symbolic objects in the stories of *FMG*, ranging from the shiny gold
tooth in the dentist's surgery in 'Un día de éstos' to the purloined
balls in 'En este pueblo no hay ladrones'. These objects tend to be
foregrounded, rather than side-lined as often happens in
Hemingway, and they are always semantically over-determined. In
'Rosas artificiales' there are three of them and they are distributed
across the three sections of the story. The first section is dominated
initially by the 'mangas', or sleeves, which are focussed on in
minute detail in the opening paragraphs and play an important
narrative role in the plot. Beyond that, we come to appreciate their
thematic import as signifiers of moral decency and the repression of
sexuality as advocated by the Church. The sleeves stand in an
antagonistic relation to the 'colorete' that besmirches Mina's face:
as an outward sign of sexual attraction, the make-up combines with
the sleeves to encapsulate the perennial conflict between nature and
culture, sexual instinct and norms of propriety, and desire and
repression, which shapes all of our lives.

Towards the end of the first section of García Márquez's
story, the sleeves give way to the bundle of letters that Mina
recovers from their hiding place in the wardrobe and throws down
the lavatory, where they will be joined, shortly after, by Trinidad's
collection of dead mice. There is an easy explanation for Mina's
ridding herself of the letters: she wishes to destroy the trail of a love
affair and to annihilate the memory of a lover who has let her down;
through his departure, their love has 'gone down the tubes', in the
English vernacular. The corpses of the mice that follow embody
additional meanings of entrapment and death which set the seal on
the story of Mina's loss and her emotional and spiritual devastation.

The third dominant motif in 'Rosas artificiales' is the roses of the title, paired with genuine roses that grow in the family garden and sharpen the thematic and emotional perspectives of the story. Excluding the title, the first roses mentioned in the story are 'las rosas del patio' (p.210), opposite which the grandmother routinely sits al fresco, drinking a cup of coffee. At the crucial point of articulation between the second and third sections of the story, the grandmother will be shown 'podando el rosal' (p.213) as Mina simultaneously dumps the mice down the lavatory. The combination of motifs here is not coincidental: the idea of wasted love (conveyed by the dumping of the mice) conflicts with the grandmother's tending to a flower that has traditionally been associated in the West with love, especially love involving sexual passion. The reader has only to think of *Le Roman de la Rose*, of Shakespeare's love poems, or the popular rhyme 'Roses are red, violets are blue...' to appreciate the rootedness of this cultural topos in the Western tradition.

Considering Mina's sorry experience, there is a cruel irony in the fact that she makes a living out of fabricating artificial roses, doing so in a workshop ('su taller de rosas artificiales') that is a metonymic condensation of her life. The narrative observes pointedly that 'Trinidad era experta en el rizado de pétalos', which seems consistent with her delicate manners and sexual primness, and reserves for Mina the job of making the wire stalks, which she then covers in a sheath of 'papel verde' (p.212). If we accept that Mina displaces her emotional and erotic impulses onto a range of more or less innocent activities (viz. the heated conversations she has with her grandmother), then her work on the rose-stalks acquires phallic connotations reminiscent of the imagery embroidered by the gypsy nun in a famous poem by Federico García Lorca:

> ¡Qué bien borda! ¡Con qué gracia!
> Sobre la tela pajiza,
> ella quisiera bordar
> flores de su fantasía.

> ¡Oh! qué llanura empinada
> con veinte soles arriba.
> ¡Qué ríos puestos de pie
> vislumbra su fantasia! (66, pp.433–34)

By analogy with the 'monja gitana', Mina's handicraft communicates with the depths of her inner life and expresses powerful emotional and sexual forces that are undeniably real.

A final association of roses with Easter time dignifies Mina's suffering by evoking no less a tragedy than Christ's passion, commemorated throughout Christendom by the placing of roses — as well as other flowers — on the altars of Catholic and Protestant churches alike in the build-up to Good Friday and Easter Sunday. The setting of the action of 'Rosas artificiales' on a Friday in Lent alerts the reader to the wider context that surrounds Mina's private passion. Mina herself makes it known that 'Son ciento cincuenta docenas de rosas que tengo que entregar en Páscua' (p.212) and then hurries to install the equipment that she and Trinidad (the name is not fortuitous) will use that morning to reduce the backlog of flowers. In case the reader fails to see the relationship between the pieces that make up García Márquez's narrative puzzle, he slips in a final clue at the very end of the story when Mina's mother, in only her second appearance in 'Rosas artificiales', 'venía por el corredor [...] cargada de ramos espinosos' (p.215). Evoking the crown of thorns placed on Christ's head during his ascent to the Cross, the image of the mother heavily laden with thorny branches also refers, artfully, to the all-too-human suffering of her only daughter, who has been abandoned by an unnamed lover on a Friday that inaugurates an uncertain future for her. This crowning poetic detail ties García Márquez to the Catholic cultural milieu about which he is writing in 'Rosas artificiales', at the same time as it underlines the assimilation of foreign artistic models such as Hemingway and Borges to his narrative project and universe.

'La viuda de Montiel':
i. Narrative structure and the woman's place

In the context of the volume under review, 'La viuda de Montiel' possesses a marked degree of structural complexity that sets it apart from all but one of the six stories commented on in the preceding pages. A crucial factor in its make-up is the inclusion of numerous passages of retrospective narration that criss-cross the linear account of the widow Montiel's troubled and lonely existence following the death of her dyspeptic husband, José. The most extreme and illuminating points of contrast within the collection are 'Rosas artificiales' and 'Un día de éstos', which concentrate exclusively on a single dimension of narrative time unbroken by any displacements or digressions. A slightly less monolithic pattern informs 'En este pueblo no hay ladrones' and 'La prodigiosa tarde de Baltazar', where a small number of references to the characters' past lives barely unsettle the predominantly linear narrative. The closest point of comparison with 'La viuda de Montiel' is 'Un día después del sábado', which evinces a shifting temporal perspective that moves back and forth over different periods in the lives of the three main characters whose paths cross in Macondo over the weekend of the story-line.

The elaborate structure of 'La viuda de Montiel' accommod-ates a narrative impulse to reconstruct the past which is the exact antithesis of the overarching design of 'Rosas artificiales': there, the controlling intelligence was determined to suppress all information about the characters' former lives, whereas in 'La viuda de Montiel' it projects the widow's immediate situation against a multi-dimensional background of personal and collective history based on 'el pueblo'. As a point of reference, the narrative provides glimpses into José Montiel and his wife's placid existence before the arrival of 'el primer alcalde de la dictadura' (p.179) —an event which Mario Vargas Llosa infers took place 'en 1945 más o menos' (28, p.381). There are certain difficulties with the Peruvian author's hypothesis, inasmuch as it fails to account for the number of years which, logically, should separate the story of 'La viuda de Montiel' from events recounted in 'La prodigiosa tarde de Baltazar'. That is where we first met don Chepe Montiel and his long-suffering wife, at a time when their son, Pepe, was a mere twelve years old. By the time Montiel dies in 'La viuda de Montiel', Pepe is fully grown and holds a consular position in Germany, from where he sends a telegram on the day of his father's burial. The insistence on 1945 (when the Second World War was still being fought on the European mainland) as the temporal benchmark for the start of a dictatorship which allowed Montiel to 'get rich quick' in a backwater in northern Colombia, has consequences for the rest of the story: Vargas Llosa's choice of date requires that Montiel die in 1951 (we are told that he had a mere six years' enjoyment of his 'desaforada riqueza', p.180); and, since his wife survives him by a further two years or so, it would bring the story of her life to a close in 1953. The apparent discrepancy between the dates of 'La viuda de Montiel' and 'La prodigiosa tarde de Baltazar' becomes a non-problem if the Montiels have more than one son, but there is no mention of such a person, and the matter of Pepe's progression to adulthood and appointment to a position in post-war Germany remains unaccounted for in Vargas Llosa's temporal scheme.

We might suppose a slightly later time-frame for 'La viuda de Montiel', one which brings the story closer to the time of writing in 1958. While such a hypothesis would be at odds with the chronology of 'La prodigiosa tarde de Baltazar' as envisioned by Vargas Llosa, it would be wholly consistent with the proposition articulated by the same critic that the temporal settings of García Márquez's narratives are fluid and governed as much by the requirement of internal consistency within a single story as by any necessary relationship between items in the set (*28*, p.345). Fortunately for the reader, there is a plethora of temporal markers in 'La viuda de Montiel' which help piece together the joint and separate stories of Montiel and his widow sketched therein. And, while no specific date is cited at any point, a letter written from Paris by Montiel's daughters abjuring Colombia as 'un país [...] salvaje donde asesinan a la gente por cuestiones políticas' (p.181) identifies the time-frame as post-1948, when the country descended into anarchy following the assassination of Jorge Eliécer Gaitán on 9 April of that year (see above, pp.50-52.).

If comparison with 'La prodigiosa tarde de Baltazar' complicates the matter of determining the precise historical parameters that might (or might not) be shared between that story and 'La viuda de Montiel', it sheds revealing light on the place of the eponymous widow within the local social order. In the earlier of the two stories, she was identified by the Christian name 'Adelaida'; when we progress to 'La viuda de Montiel', we find that the individualising detail of a name has been revoked or forgotten, and the character's identity subsumed under the label of 'Montiel's widow'. The story begins with a lengthy paragraph that fixes on the corpse and burial of don José and makes not so much as a single mention of Adelaida, who begins to come into her own only in the second and third paragraphs. Thereafter, her story alternates with retrospective narration on the subject of her husband's rise to economic power through an alliance with the local mayor which worked by expelling all the rich entrepreneurs from the town and concentrating wealth in the hands of Montiel. Only in the last two pages (out of a total of fewer than eight) does the narrative of her solitude take pride of place, to the exclusion of any other material. At that point, a full year has elapsed since Montiel's death and another will follow, at the end of which Adelaida will receive a letter from her daughters with a colourful phrase that brings a smile to her lips 'por primera vez en dos años' (p.182). With that, the narrative will follow the widow up the stairs to her bedroom and into a state of sleep which may end in death; at the very least, it provides an oneiric framework for a hallucinatory encounter with Mamá Grande, a legendary figure rooted in local superstition, in whom the widow plainly believes.

The fact that the eponymous widow has to contend from the start for narrative space with her dead husband is a telling comment on her status as a subordinate whose subjectivity was threatened by her husband's bullying whilst he was alive and becomes increasingly fragile after his death. Adelaida begins the process of adjustment to her new circumstances three days after the removal of

Montiel's corpse from the house, but 'el rumbo de su nueva vida' (p.176) runs up against problems of temperament and circumstance. Two months of grieving indoors instil in her 'la costumbre de morderse las uñas' (p.177), which becomes a sign of neurosis and necessitates the nightly binding of 'la uña del pulgar derecho, irritada por los mordiscos' (p.182). The narrative associates the biting of nails with feeding off resentment, and this accurately sums up the widow's unhealthy emotional condition and outlook.

Circumstances also conspire to make life a misery for her. The inheritance of her husband's 'desordenada y fabulosa hacienda' (p.177) comes to nought as the townsfolk boycott the family's business interests in reprisal for Montiel's many past abuses. The narrative acknowledges the widow's disgust at the mayor and his barbaric regime, but the people deem her guilty of complicity in its murderous and corrupt practices and make her pay for her husband's venal behaviour. Crucially, her son lets it be known that he does not dare return from Germany to take charge of the family's business empire, 'por temor de que le dieran un tiro'. This news is the trigger for the long-serving administrator, Mr Carmichael, to advise Mrs Montiel that 'se estaba quedando en la ruina' (p.181). He is described as 'un negro viejo, de piel lustrosa, vestido de blanco' (p. 177) who would tempt fate by always entering the house with his umbrella open. The only man to set foot there after Montiel's death, he is effectively a messenger of doom, whose final words seal the fate both of the widow, who declares herself 'hasta la coronilla de quesos y moscas' (emblems of the corruption that surrounds her, p.181), and of the family businesses, which are not referred to again in the story.

ii. The widow, framed

The final section of the narrative is set in train by the widow's parting words to Carmichael, 'Si usted quiere, llévese lo que le haga falta y déjeme morir tranquila'. From that moment on, we are told, 'su único contacto con el mundo [...] fueron las cartas que escribía a sus hijas a fines de cada mes' (p.181). To be sure, there is a certain pathos in the situation of a woman, now in her mid-sixties, whose prevailing air throughout her marriage, according to the narrative of 'La prodigiosa tarde de Baltazar, was one of 'quieto patetismo' (p.171), and who has since descended into neurosis and a state of mind riddled with superstition and resentment. If we add to all that the collapse of her husband's business empire and her son's refusal to come home to help salvage it, then we are entitled to feel a certain sympathy for Adelaida and to regard her seclusion from the world about her, and her cultivation of the bond with her absent daughters, as wholly understandable in the circumstances. Against this charitable reading, we sense more than a hint of disapproval on the author's part for a woman who displays levels of snobbery and ignorance equalled only by Sra. Rebeca in 'Un día después del sábado' and, at a later stage in García Márquez's oeuvre, by Fernanda del Carpio in *Cien años de soledad.*

The letters exchanged with her daughters in Paris carry within them the seeds of the widow's defamation. We become privy to the contents of only one letter that she writes, and the impression that it creates is mixed. On the one hand, the widow anathematizes the town where she lives as 'un pueblo maldito', giving vent to resentment and prejudice; on the other hand, she tells her daughters, 'Quédense allá para siempre y no se preocupen por mí. Yo soy feliz sabiendo que ustedes son felices' (p.181). This last remark renders acutely the attitude of many a mother who puts the happiness of her children ahead of her own, in the purest spirit of self-sacrifice and love; there is nevertheless a sub-text of self-justification and guilt-tripping in the widow's discourse that is less admirable.

The narrative provides a fuller account of the letters sent by the daughters, along with valuable insight into the widow's response which eventually undoes her in the reader's eyes. The letters centre, in the first instance, on the daughters' preference for living in Paris rather than Colombia: '"Esto es la civilización", decían. "Allá, en cambio, no es un buen medio para nosotras. Es imposible vivir en un país donde asesinan a la gente por cuestiones políticas"'(p.181). Without denying the truly barbaric realities of political violence in Colombia around the time of writing, the passage dramatises, in tell-tale fashion, the parroting of an ideology that identifies the Old World (represented paradigmatically by Paris) with 'civilisation' and the New World with 'barbarism', after Eurocentric prejudices that arguably reached their peak in the middle of the nineteenth century. Those prejudices found their way, with certain adjustments, into the writings of various contemporary Latin American thinkers including, most emblematically, Domingo Faustino Sarmiento (1811–88) in his essay, *Civilización y barbarie: vida de Juan Facundo Quiroga* (1848). A counter-tradition within Latin American thought and letters would be spearheaded by figures including Simón Bolívar, 'El Libertador', who was born in Caracas, New Spain, in 1783 and died in northern Colombia in 1830, José Martí (Cuba 1853–95) and Leopoldo Zea (Mexico b.1912), who rejected the implications for the Americas of the civilisation/barbarism binary and, in the case of Zea, turned the terms around and attached the label of civilisation to the peoples and cultures of Spanish America.

Crucially, the ideological and political defence of the Americas is something to which García Márquez has pledged allegiance throughout his career. Amongst the most notable expressions of this position are his address on accepting the Nobel Prize for Literature in Stockholm in 1983, and the words that he puts into the mouth of the ailing but feisty Simón Bolívar in conversation with the opinionated Frenchman, Diocles Atlantique, near the half-way mark of *El general en su laberinto* (1989). With the benefit of hindsight, we can recognise the identification, by Montiel's daughters, of Paris/France/Europe with 'civilisation' as one of the very first instances of the fictional (as opposed to the journalistic) treatment of this theme in Márquez's oeuvre. The daughters' parroting of a long-established imperialistic discourse is an illustration of their internalisation of Eurocentric and anti-American prejudice, and a warning to the reader to mistrust their motives. In fact, the passage that is quoted from one of their letters is preceded by a critical gloss which informs us, 'Sus cartas eran siempre alegres, y se veía que habían sido escritas en lugares tibios y bien iluminados y que las muchachas se veían repetidas en muchos espejos cuando se detenían a pensar' (p.181). Both Harley

Oberhelman and George McMurray detect a reference here to Hemingway's 'A Clean, Well-lighted Place' (*23*, pp.36–38; *20*, p.54), and draw conclusions consonant with that premise. For my part, I find it more productive to focus on the imagery of mirrors and to see in the description of the daughters' location a staging of inauthentic identity, nicely captured in the repetition, in García Márquez's own prose, of the construction, 'se veía' / 'se veían'. Read this way, the sentence underscores the complexity of the various processes, conscious and unconscious, that contribute to the formation of identity, and does not hold back from suggesting that the daughters are morally self-deluding and politically dishonest.

From the point of view of the presentation of their mother, the passage cited from the daughters' letter is primarily of interest because of her response: 'Leyendo las cartas, la viuda de Montiel se sentía mejor y aprobaba cada frase con la cabeza' (p. 181). Coming at the very end of the paragraph that reproduced the daughters' views on civilisation, this sentence tars Adelaida Montiel with the same ideological brush as them. In popular parlance, the daughters and the mother alike are caught in the act of self-incrimination by a narrator who uses techniques of reported speech, obliqueness and irony to frame all three of them.

The contents of another letter further compromise Montiel's widow, whose innocent but unthinking reaction to what she reads backfires on her. The narrative account is lengthy and multi-layered and merits quoting in full:

> En cierta ocasión, sus hijas le hablaron de los mercados de carne de París. Le decían que mataban unos cerdos rosados y los colgaban enteros en la puerta adornados con coronas y guirnaldas de flores. Al final, una letra diferente a la de sus hijas había agregado: 'Imagínate, que el clavel más grande y más bonito se lo ponen al cerdo en el culo.' Leyendo aquella frase, por primera vez en dos años, la viuda de Montiel sonrió. (pp.181–82)

Imagery of butchery has a sharply-delineated history in modern Spanish American literature, going back to 'El matadero' by Esteban Echeverría (Argentina 1805–51) where it dramatised the barbaric violence inflicted on a naïve political dissident by thugs working for the strongman, Juan Manuel Rosas.[2] By sarcastically translating a seminal, and indeed paradigmatic image of South American barbarism across time and space to the Paris of the 1950s, the quoted passage undermines claims that would continue to associate Paris/France/Europe with civilisation either at the height of European imperialism (viz. the missions ordered by Emperor Napoleon III to areas such as North Africa and Mexico in the 1860s) or at the beginning of its decline in the aftermath of World War II nearly a century later. The reference to 'mercados de carne en París', therefore, cuts both ways in connection with the issues raised by the daughters in the monthly letters they write to their mother back home in Colombia.

Ironically and poignantly, the slaughter-house motif possesses its keenest relevance in relation to the violence perpetrated in Colombia from 1948 on and in the 'pueblo' where José Montiel made his fortune. The graphic report supplied by Montiel's daughters, of pigs' carcasses hung 'enteros en la puerta adornados con coronas y guirnaldas de flores' (p. 181), refers the attentive reader back to the opening paragraphs of 'La viuda de Montiel' and to the description of don José's corpse laid out 'en cámara ardiente, embutido con almohadas y sábanas de lino dentro de una caja amarilla y abombada como un melón' (p. 175). Apart from the unusual occurrence of a simile in the author's prose (where there is often not a single simile in a story and rarely more than two in the longer stories under consideration), the critical element in the opening description of don José is the metaphor, 'embutido', which equates him with pig's meat, or tripe. The clever characterisation of him as so much dead meat is strengthened by the reference to the floral wreaths sent on the occasion of his funeral, when his widow 'esperaba que la casa fuera pequeña para recibir tantas flores' and is

---

[2] By common assent, the story was written around 1849/50 but not published until 1871, almost a quarter of a century after the author's death.

disappointed to receive no more 'coronas que las de la administra-
ción municipal' (p. 176). The web of imagery associates don José
with pigs (the narrative confirms that he was an 'hombre gordo',
p.179) and barbarism, and plays an uncharitable trick on his widow
by making her ludicrously blind to the political implications of the
comment added by an anonymous hand to the daughters' colourful
description of the pigs. The anonymous scribe imagines a carnation
being stuck up each pig's arse, which the widow finds strangely
amusing. However, she is plainly ignorant of the symbolic violation
of her husband's dignity that this image represents, and she does not
bother to question the motivation behind the added comment. Since
the anonymous words were written in Spanish, we have to assume
that their author is a citizen of the pueblo who intercepts the
daughters' letter and adds an obscenity out of personal spite and in
revenge for Montiel's alliance with the local 'butchers' who carried
out 'la matanza política' (p. 178) that decimated the population of
the town some years earlier. The widow thus becomes the butt of
narrative irony (pun intended), since she actually laughs at a
comment which debases her husband's memory, 'dándole por el
culo' in a verbal gesture of sexualised violence.

iii. Enter la Mamá Grande...

The vicious turn that the story takes in the penultimate and final
paragraphs predisposes the reader to react circumspectly to the
closing scene where Montiel's widow has a vision of Mamá Grande.
As documented in the Introduction to this Guide, García Márquez
had in the early 1950s written a set of essays about 'un país de
leyenda dentro de la costa atlántica de Colombia', giving pride of
place to a figure known as 'la Marquesita' who, he explained, 'era
una especie de gran mamá de quienes le servían en la Sierpe' (5, II,
p.119). The appearance of Mamá Grande at the very end of 'La
viuda de Montiel' brings this character for the first time out of the
realm of pseudo-anthropological reportage into the more literary but
no less imaginative parameters of narrative fiction.

    In contrast to the fuller development of the theme one year
later in the title story of *FMG*, 'La viuda de Montiel' offers a partial

and momentary glimpse of the legendary Marquesita, poised in a liminal space between the enigmatic conclusion of one story and the beginning of another. The conclusion to 'La viuda de Montiel' is enigmatic on two counts: first, because of the imagery that accompanies Mamá Grande, and second, because of the ambiguous implications of the few words she says to Montiel's widow. The narrative context is as follows: the widow has gone up to her bedroom and has begun to count the rosary beads, which she shifts from her right to her left hand, 'pues no sentía las cuentas a través del esparadrapo [en] la uña del pulgar derecho'. She falls asleep and has a vision of Mamá Grande 'en el patio con una sábana blanca y un peine en el regazo, destripando piojos con los pulgares'. In a short exchange, the widow asks Mamá Grande when she is going to die, and Mamá Grande answers, 'Cuando te empiece el cansancio del brazo' (182). What is ambiguous about her answer is the possibility that the process of 'el cansancio del brazo' foreseen by Mamá Grande has already begun. The narrative tells us that Montiel's widow's right thumb is numb, necessitating a change of hand in order to feel the rosary beads; it does not say openly that she is dying, but it raises that possibility through ambiguity.

The imagery of lice being gutted or disembowelled identifies Mamá Grande as a 'taker away of life', in Erich Neumann's typology of features of the Great Mother archetype (75, p.197). Within the immediate confines of the story, the verbal form 'destripando' eerily evokes the motif of pig meat or 'embutidos' applied earlier to José Montiel and hints at a connection between Mamá Grande and his death. This proposition is consistent with the narrative indication that she possesses supernatural knowledge of death — a faculty taken for granted by the widow in her routine dealings with Mamá Grande. However, we must not overlook the fact that the entire episode, including the dialogue that Montiel's widow holds with Mamá Grande, occurs within the frame of a dream and/or hallucination, which places the emphasis of the passage as much on issues of ideology and belief as on the mechanics of representation. The result is that our attention turns once more to the mind-set of Montiel's widow, which has already been criticised as a site of sickness, ignorance and prejudice.

Through the narrative of her oneiric encounter with Mamá Grande, the widow's mental state is rendered in greater detail than before and assimilates to the type of the neurotic old woman exemplified by Sra. Rebeca, the 'viuda amargada' of 'Un día después del sábado' and elsewhere. In the case of 'La viuda de Montiel' the determining factors in the development of the eponymous character's neurosis are i) a parental upbringing that for twenty years kept Adelaida away from 'contacto directo con la realidad', and ii) susceptibility to superstition: the early description of her as 'Aquella mujer frágil, lacerada por la superstición' (p. 176) sums up her character perfectly and paves the way for the narrative of her encounter with Mamá Grande, which takes place in an atmosphere of perfect naturalness. The episode thus provides compelling evidence that the widow has internalised the image of Mamá Grande, who occupies an important place in her mental world. This consideration is crucial, not only for our understanding of 'La viuda de Montiel' but also as a preparation for the final story in the collection, where Mamá Grande moves to centre stage. If the presence of such a figure in 'La viuda de Montiel' expands the scope of the author's realism by accommodating an element of popular culture belonging to the area of La Sierpe, it also serves the purpose of laying bare the ideological structures that make up a people's mind-set, which can then be analysed in the light of several factors, including considerations relating to political morality and history. In the next chapter, I will follow this perception through as a tool for interpreting 'Los funerales de la Mamá Grande', which builds on this and numerous other elements from 'La viuda de Montiel' as it elaborates a mordant critique of traditional institutions and attitudes in contemporary Spanish American society.

6. 'Los funerales de la Mamá Grande':
the Death of the Old and the Birth of the New

i. Introduction

The narrative depiction of the figure of Mamá Grande crystallises most fully in this story which was written, according to Dasso Saldívar, in May and June 1959 (*2*, p.386). The legendary matriarch of La Sierpe who appeared in a dream to Montiel's widow in her house in the *pueblo* is re-figured here as 'soberana absoluta del reino de Macondo' (p.216), in a pen-portrait which ties her to the setting of two earlier stories already discussed in Chapter Two of this Guide. The mention of real place-names such as La Guajira and Aracataca also identifies Mamá Grande explicitly with the *costa* region of northern Colombia and paves the way for the later expansion of the story's geographical frame of reference to take in the site of national government in Bogotá and, somewhat improbably, the official and summer residences of the Pope in Italy. Mamá Grande's story is also contextualised within broader historical parameters extending back into Spanish American colonial history and down to the present day where it picks up on both national and international events: a press report about the finding of a young woman's headless body on the lake-side at Castelgandolfo, near the Pope's summer residence, belongs to the world of real events that García Márquez covered as a reporter working for the Colombian newspaper *El Espectador* in Europe in 1955, and anchors the story in a precise moment of contemporary history (*5*, IV, p.128).

At the same time as it fills out Mamá Grande's geographical and historical profile, the story that carries her name converts her into a figure that is literally larger than life and the focal point of comic hyperbole. An unprecedented feature of the story in relation to all those that precede it is the presence of a highly conspicuous narrative voice that is disrespectful and satirical in the treatment it metes out to its subjects. An analysis of the narrative of 'Los funerales de la Mamá Grande' must take into account the varied tone and multiple orientations of a story which uses irony, satire and black humour to address issues of life and death, power and politics, and stagnation and renewal. In its literary construction, 'Los funerales de la Mamá Grande' employs narrative structure, point of view, parody, hyperbole, and allegory to criticise the historical failings of political classes and institutions in a fictional realm ('el reino de Macondo', p. 216) whose resemblance to the situation in central and northern Colombia is taken for granted by both Jacques Gilard (*5*, IV, p.71) and Luis Carlos Herrera Molina (*17*, p.121). Echoes from an earlier narrative by Jorge Zalamea, *El gran Burundún-Burundá ha muerto* (1952), confirm the geo-political parameters of 'Los funerales de la Mamá Grande' and provide a yardstick for measuring the extent to which García Márquez can be credited with the creation of a distinctive narrative style and vision.

ii. *Framing the story of la Mamá Grande*

Not for the first time in the collection, the story of a named main character is set within a narrative frame comprising, on this occasion, a single page of two introductory paragraphs and one concluding paragraph of slightly greater length. The narrative opens as follows:

> Esta es, incrédulos del mundo entero, la verídica historia de la Mamá Grande, soberana absoluta del reino de Macondo, que vivió en función de dominio durante 92 años y murió en olor de santidad un martes del setiembre pasado, y a cuyos funerales vino el Sumo Pontífice. (p. 216)

From the very start, we are addressed as universal readers and challenged to accept as historical truth an account about a fictional character who has just died after nearly a century of sovereign rule

over the realm of Macondo. The inordinate length of the supposed
monarch's rule raises suspicions about narrative exaggeration and
credibility, which are not allayed by the claim that Mamá Grande's
funeral was attended by no less a personage than the Pope. By the
end of the first sentence, the reader senses ironic possibilities in the
narrator's appeal to the incredulous of the world: on the one hand,
the story that he is telling about Mamá Grande is a tall story that
invites a rightly incredulous response; on the other, it may contain
elements of sufficient truthfulness (the narrator introduces it
expressly as a 'verídica historia') to warrant a reading based on
trust.

The second of the two introductory paragraphs elaborates on
the issue of truthfulness and the moral and intellectual imperative to
respect historical fact. Before doing that, however, it invokes the
different frames of reference that the narrative wishes to bring into
play, from the local and regional, through the national, to the
universal. The narrative privileges the local and regional frame of
reference over the national, with types including 'los gaiteros de
San Jacinto, los contrabandistas de la Guajira' and 'las prostitutas
de Guacamayal' outnumbering and overshadowing the colourless
representatives of government in the nation's capital. The raising of
local smugglers and prostitutes to the same level of importance as
the Head of State makes the reader think immediately of the
atmosphere of carnival and the world turned upside down.
Hierarchies are then collapsed once more with the juxtaposition of
high and low, Heaven and earth, in the clause, 'ahora que el Sumo
Pontífice ha subido a los Cielos en cuerpo y alma y que es imposible
transitar en Macondo a causa de las botellas vacías, las colillas de
cigarrillos, los huesos roídos', etc. Through these ploys, the narrative
seeks to evoke 'la más espléndida ocasión funeraria que registren
los anales históricos' (p. 216), appealing to a pride in local life and
culture that is expressed in other writings by García Márquez,
including the essays that he wrote about La Sierpe some seven years
before the composition of 'Los funerales de la Mamá Grande'.

Having set the scene of the aftermath of the matriarch's
funeral, the narrative voice proclaims that the moment has arrived

when 'es la hora de recostar un taburete a la puerta de la calle y empezar a contar desde el principio los pormenores de esta conmoción nacional antes de que tengan tiempo de llegar los historiadores' (pp.216–17). Essential elements here are i) the image that the narrator conveys of popular story-telling in a public, oral style and ii) the pre-empting of official versions of history through the creation of a more popular and locally-based alternative. Official historiography is something that the narrator views with suspicion; what he has to offer in its stead is more immediate and fresh and, he implies, more truthful than official history. His claims sound ambitious, to be sure, but they are nonetheless likely to find favour with those who share his political sentiments. Such a clearly defined and partisan stance prepares the reader of 'Los funerales de la Mamá Grande' for a story that promises to be lively and polemical.

iii. Perspectives on the past

After the exposition, the narrative content of 'Los funerales de la Mamá Grande' falls into two roughly symmetrical parts, the first of which dwells on the final hours of the dying matriarch up until the moment when she 'emitió un sonoro eructo, y expiró' (p. 226). Thereafter, the focus shifts to the preparations and actual celebration of Mamá Grande's funeral, before eventually returning to the fictional present of narration, which post-dates the matriarch's death by some fourteen weeks and her funeral by a further, unspecified amount of time. As happened in 'La viuda de Montiel', the linear axis of the narrative is broken, especially in the first half of 'Los funerales de la Mamá Grande', by reconstructions of the matriarch's personal and family history going back several generations. The figure of two hundred years is cited twice as proof of the family's historic grip on power, amounting to 'una hegemonía que colmaba dos siglos' (p.218). On the basis that the fictional present of Mamá Grande's death is post-1955 (viz. the newspaper report about the finding of a decapitated female body at Castelgandolfo), this early temporal reference traces the beginnings of the family's influence back to the middle of the eighteenth century and to colonial Spanish rule. The narrative obligingly confirms, apropos the origins of the family estate, that 'el patrimonio físico se reducía a tres encomiendas adjudicadas por Cédula Real durante la Colonia, y que con el transcurso del tiempo, en virtud de intrincados matrimonios de conveniencia, se habían acumulado bajo el dominio de la Mamá Grande' (p.223). We remember the legend of la Marquesita de la Sierpe, who was of Spanish origins and lived 'más de doscientos años' (5, II, p.120); in relation to other stories in the volume, Mamá Grande's ancestors would have belonged to the same ideological class as the paternal family of Sra. Rebeca, the 'viuda amargada' of 'Un día después del sábado', whose great-grandfather was a loyal subject of the Spanish Crown and, after the wars of Independence, travelled to Spain 'con el propósito exclusivo de visitar el palacio que construyó Carlos III en San Ildefonso' (p. 183).

Mamá Grande's personal history is less susceptible to exact reconstruction. The narrative mentions a photograph of her in her twenties 'captada por un fotógrafo ambulante que pasó por Macondo a principios de siglo' (p. 226), which would suggest a date of birth around 1880. It is impossible, however, to square this with the opening claim that Mamá Grande dies after ninety two years 'en función de dominio' (p. 216), and the reader concludes that dates and figures provided at various points in the story are approximate and elastic. At first sight, this proviso does not seem to apply to the report of a key event in the matriarch's life, which took place when she was twenty two years of age. The occasion was her own father's funeral, which marked her elevation to the position of Mamá Grande: 'Los ancianos recordaban [...] la tarde en que María del Rosario Castañeda y Montero asistió a los funerales de su padre, y regresó por la calle esterada investida de su nueva e irradiante dignidad, a los 22 años convertida en la Mamá Grande'. However, that momentous change in status resulted in the young woman's entry into the realm of legend and myth, where she remained thereafter: 'Cada vez más imprecisa y remota, visible apenas en su balcón sofocado entonces por los geranios en las tardes de calor, la Mamá Grande se esfumaba en su propia leyenda' (p. 221). This consideration helps explain the imprecision of many references to time in the story, and points up their value as indicators of the archetypal cast of the matriarch's personality and regime. The profiles of two minor characters, Mamá Grande's centenarian priest, father Antonio Isabel, and her gun-toting nephew, Nicanor, demonstrate the workings of the story's symbolic design: drawn flimsily, to the point of caricature, the two men, who are also relatives, appear as transparent ciphers of the institutions of the Catholic Church, in the first case, and, in that of Nicanor, of *caciquismo* (local bossism) and the military, whose collective support was vital to the oligarchies that ran the affairs of many Spanish American countries from the earliest years of Independence, lasting, in some cases, right down to the time of writing in 1959.

'Los funerales de la Mamá Grande' draws particular attention to the importance of the land in the accumulation of power by Mamá Grande's forebears. Measuring approximately one hundred hectares, the land would have remained fallow but for their decision to rent it out piecemeal to three hundred and fifty two families who would put it to productive use. This arrangement guaranteed Mamá Grande income in the form of rent and a proportion of the agricultural output, at the same time as it prevented the State from reclaiming the land. The concentration, within her domain, of the six prosperous boroughs ('poblaciones') of the district of Macondo brought additional benefits in the form of tax revenue on buildings and payments that the government was obliged to make 'por el uso que los ciudadanos hacían en las calles'. Through these and other 'circunstancias históricas', or accidents of history, Mamá Grande's economic resources and her power base appear as a distorted version of the Spanish colonial heritage in the Americas, further imaged as a stash of treasure 'enterra[do] en algún lugar de la casa durante la Guerra de Independencia' and never found, in spite of excavations carried out by successive generations of family members (p. 224).

iv. Mamá Grande's moral patrimony

The physical boundaries and foundations of Mamá Grande's estate are buttressed by her claim to a set of 'bienes morales' which she enumerates on her death-bed. In the end, the 'goods' are so numerous that she is unable to complete the list and she dies of congestion, rather like Funes 'el memorioso' in a famous story by Jorge Luis Borges. Mamá Grande's 'patrimonio invisible' mixes up institutional, material, political, and philosophical categories such as the nation's territorial waters and the colours of the flag, human rights, free elections, the supreme court of justice, linguistic purity, the ship of state, and republican traditions, in a sprawling list of no fewer than forty items that mimics the matriarch's indiscriminate appetite for moral and political control. The passage abounds in humour deriving from incongruous juxtapositions and relentless satire — especially of the rhetoric and ideology of a conservative class identified quintessentially, in García Márquez's mind, with the Colombian capital, Bogotá ('la Atenas sudamericana', p.225). But the narrator also makes the serious point that the appropriation, by Mamá Grande and her cronies, of the ideals and catchwords of democracy along with the values and slogans of a stagnant and reactionary conservatism gave moral legitimacy to a centuries-long stranglehold on power.

The narrator's point about moral legitimacy ('la justificación moral', p. 226) opens up the question of who might be responsible for a regime of hegemony and privilege that has endured so long. Speaking in his real voice, and no longer ventriloquising as Mamá Grande, the narrator devotes considerable space to criticizing the national authorities for their historical connivance in the dynastic abuse of power. Mamá Grande's direct involvement in violent and illegal practices including armed support for warring political factions and rampant electoral fraud, does not deter the ruling classes from regarding her as their ally. In their view, 'Ella era la prioridad del poder tradicional sobre la autoridad transitoria, el predominio de la clase sobre la plebe, la trascendencia de la sabiduría divina sobre la improvisación mortal' (p.227). As soon as he learns of her death, the Head of State orders nine days of national mourning and solemnly ascribes Mamá Grande to 'la categoría de heroína muerta por la patria en el campo de batalla' (p.228).

That the representatives of national institutions should side
with the defenders of local tradition and inherited privilege is
perhaps to be expected, along with the satirical barbs directed by the
narrator against the figure of the president and that of Mamá
Grande. A more interesting aspect of his assessment of Mamá
Grande's anachronistic regime is his criticism of the role of the
common people in its historical operations and continuity. For,
whilst it cannot be denied that the people have been victims of what
is de facto a feudal abuse of power, they are, the narrator suggests,
also guilty of complicity in their own repression and mystification.
He makes this point early on in his narration when he says, 'Nadie
conocía el origen, ni los límites, ni el valor real del patrimonio, pero
todo el mundo se había acostumbrado a creer que la Mamá Grande
era dueña de las aguas corrientes y estancadas, llovidas y por llover,
y de los caminos vecinales, los postes del telégrafo, los años
bisiestos y el calor, y que tenía además un derecho heredado sobre
vida y haciendas' (p.218). Custom and belief are determining
factors in the persistence of the status quo, including belief in the
most irrational and ridiculous propositions such as Mamá Grande's
'ownership' — natural, and therefore incontestable — of past and
future rainfall and leap-years — just two of many absurdities that
are attributed to the *pueblo* by one who knows its motivations,
including nostalgia for an aristocratic order, its prejudices and, most
damagingly, its moral and rational deficiencies. The point is
reinforced in the following paragraph: 'A nadie se le había ocurrido
pensar que la Mamá Grande fuera mortal' (p.219).

The position of the narrator within this critique is complex
and many-sided. Because he identifies with *costa* culture, he resists
the centralizing impulses of national authority and feels proud that
no less a personage than the Pope should visit 'el reino de la
balsamina y de la iguana' (p.231) to play a cameo role in the
greatest spectacle ever seen in Macondo. Regionalist sentiment goes
so far as to align the narrator with that dimension of Mamá
Grande's persona which makes her a symbol of *costa* worth and
glory. However, he offers few apologies for the ordinary people of
Macondo and fewer still for their exploitative sovereign, Mamá

Grande. In his presentation of the matriarch, the narrator exploits a full range of carnivalesque techniques to diminish her aura and demystify the legends that help maintain her grip on power. Principally, he centres attention on her massive physique, which he subjects to some vicious, if colourful jibes. An early image represents Mamá Grande taking the evening air on the terrace, 'con todo el peso de sus vísceras y su autoridad aplastado en su viejo mecedor' (pp.218–19). Contempt takes on openly misogynous inflections in a later scene of the old woman stretched out on her death bed, with barely a sign of life detectable 'en la tenue respiración de sus tetas matriarcales'. At this point, the narrator chooses to elaborate: 'La Mamá Grande [...], que fue dotada por la naturaleza para amamantar ella sola a toda su especie, agonizaba virgen y sin hijos' (p.222) — a condemnation of instinctual denial and sterility that may be explained in part as relaying popular hostility toward the matriarch, but whose vulgarity and vindictiveness are none the less remarkable for that.

v. Humour and the body politic

The resounding belch that issues from Mamá Grande's outsize frame at the moment of her death marks the end of the first half of the narrative and ushers in the second with an immediate shift of setting to Bogotá; the narrative then moves on to Rome and finally comes back to Macondo on the eve of the matriarch's funeral service. The explosion of a loud bodily indiscretion sets the tone for several pages of satire and black humour that revolve around the image of Mamá Grande's corpse, rotting at 40 degrees in the Caribbean shade, and the bureaucratic stuffiness of the authorities in Bogotá, who take weeks to approve a constitutional amendment designed to allow the president of the Republic to attend the matriarch's funeral. Several pages of narrative (more than the total length of 'Un día de éstos', for example) are given over to describing the atmosphere and politics of 'la capital remota y sombría', where 'una llovizna menuda cubría de recelo y de verdín a los transeúntes' (p.226). The centres of power and decision-making in 'el Capitolio Nacional' are degraded by the presence of 'mendigos envueltos en papeles [quienes] dormían al amparo de columnas dóricas y taciturnas estatuas de presidentes muertos' (p.227); in the chambers of Congress, 'horas interminables' were filled with debate which the narrator derides as 'blablablá histórico'; and, when 'alguien dotado de sentido de la realidad' pointed out the inconvenience of delaying the interment of Mamá Grande's corpse, 'Nadie se inmutó frente a aquella irrupción del sentido común en la atmósfera pura de la ley escrita' (p.229). Besides exemplifying coldness and poverty, therefore, Bogotá represents the sterility of patriarchal law and stands in opposition to the warmth and vitality of northern climes, home to a vibrant popular oral culture and the narrator's flamboyant spoken discourse.

The page or so that is devoted to Rome and the Pope displays a number of features, of which humour is the most conspicuous and varied. At the start the narrative radiates an air of charming improbability, based on the premise that Mamá Grande was known to the Pope and his cardinals who, as soon as they read about her death, determine that the Holy Father should travel to Macondo and attend the funeral in person. With the narrative of the journey, the story enters the realm of the fantastic in its treatment of time and space: instead of catching a plane, the Pope boards a 'larga góndola negra' and sails to 'los dominios de la Gran Vieja', which might be credible if it were not for the circumstance that his 'canoa pontificia' covers thousands of nautical miles in the space of just one night! This impossible 'itinerario nocturno' takes the Pope across the line of demarcation that separates 'el Imperio Romano y los hatos de la Mamá Grande', where he is hailed by men and women 'que abandonaban sus ocupaciones habituales para tentar fortuna con cosas de vender en los funerales' (p.230) and join him on the last leg of the trip.

Once he has arrived in Macondo, the Pope pointedly has to wait like everybody else for the final arrangements for the funeral to be put in place. Taking advantage of the prolonged delay, which is reckoned to last 'semanas interminables y meses alargados por la expectativa y el calor', the narrator obliges the Pope to assimilate to local life, which he does by giving 'caramelos italianos a los niños que se acercaban a verlo por la ventana' (p. 231) and by routinely taking lunch with father Antonio Isabel. These humorous touches work, in large part, as further instances of the collapsing of hierarchies and a strategic repositioning of the notional centre at the margins. In terms of aesthetics, the narrative of the Pope's translation to American soil is an example in miniature of magical-realist narration — which is something I deal with at greater length below.

On the long-awaited day of Mamá Grande's funeral the narra-tive reprises some of its earlier themes, especially the celebration of local types and values, and makes renewed use of the rhetoric of hyperbole, mock-epic and the satire of officialdom. It grants special prominence to the corpse of Mamá Grande which is described, first, prostrate 'bajo un estremecido promontorio de telegramas' (p.231) and then inside a coffin sealed with 'ocho torniquetes de cobre', where the matriarch lies saturated 'en su eternidad de formaldehído' (p.233). References to 'splendour' and 'homage' notwithstanding, the prevailing tone of the narrative at this point is tongue in cheek and no more respectful to Mamá Grande than it had been to the corpse of José Montiel in the preceding story, where the unsympathetic narration of the passing of a corrupt and porcine individual can be seen clearly in retrospect as anticipating the narrative situation and ideological design of 'Los funerales de la Mamá Grande'.

vi. Closing the frame around 'Los funerales de la Mamá Grande'

The linear narrative of García Márquez's story remains incomplete without the burial of the (now mummified) matriarch, and confirmation of this appears a few lines before the story's end. The narrative voice that had opened 'Los funerales de la Mamá Grande' reasserts its distinctive tone and presence in the final paragraph, where it echoes and elaborates on several motifs that featured in the exposition. With Mamá Grande finally laid to rest 'bajo una plataforma de plomo', the narrator concludes,

> Sólo faltaba entonces que alguien recostara un taburete
> en la puerta para contar esta historia, lección y
> escarmiento de las generaciones futuras, y que ninguno
> de los incrédulos del mundo se quedara sin conocer la
> noticia de la Mamá Grande, que mañana miércoles
> vendrán los barrenderos y barrerán la basura de sus
> funerales, por todos los siglos de los siglos. (pp.234–35)

A striking difference here from the style of the introductory
paragraphs is the absence of verbs in the present tense, which had
been conspicuous in the opening sentence: 'Esta es [...] la verídica
historia de la Mamá Grande', and in the accompanying statement,
'Ahora es la hora de recostar un taburete a la puerta de la calle [...]'
(pp.216–17). The projection of attention, at the end of the narrative,
onto two differentiated futures presupposes a notional present from
which that projection is made, but the present tense is nowhere to be
seen. The pattern of tenses in the final paragraph starts with the
preterite in the sequence, 'Obnubilado por el espectáculo del poder,
el populacho no determinó el ávido aleteo [...]', 'Nadie vio [...] ni
reparó [...]', 'Nadie advirtió [...]', and 'Lo único que para nadie
pasó inadvertido [...] fue [...]', and then moves into the imperfect
tense for the sentence beginning 'Ahora podía el Sumo Pontífice
subir al cielo [...]' and the final sentence as quoted in the inset
above. The overwhelming effect of this pattern is to emphasize the
imaginative gap that separates the moment of enunciation, on the
eve of 'mañana miércoles' (p.235), from the axis of events that have
culminated in the funeral service for Mamá Grande. That gap may
be measured in units as small as hours or a half-day, but it
represents a crucial conceptual distance separating the narrator from
the material that he has divulged over the course of the narrative.
For one thing, it allows him to account for the immediate aftermath
of the matriarch's funeral, which sheds significant light on the
behaviour of some of the characters involved in the story; for
another, it outlines a critical position that the reader is invited to
occupy, standing alongside the narrator and sharing his privileged

perspective on the historical and ideological issues that surround the figure and story of Mamá Grande.

A crucial point in the narrator's concluding remarks concerns blindness on the part of 'el populacho' to a good deal of what is going on around them. Significantly, the people remain 'obnubilado' by the spectacle of power. They do not notice 'la vigilante sombra de gallinazos que siguió al cortejo por las ardientes callecitas de Macondo', nor are they aware of the concerted action of 'los sobrinos, ahijados, sirvientes y protegidos de la Mamá Grande' who dismantle her house and share out the pieces amongst themselves. According to the narrator, just a few individuals recognise the ultimate significance and historical importance of the situation: 'Algunos de los allí presentes dispusieron de la suficiente clarividencia para comprender que estaban asistiendo al nacimiento de una nueva época' (p.234). This is consistent both with a Marxist assessment of the role of intellectuals regarding the historical process and with the deep scepticism about the common people that is expressed earlier on in 'Los funerales de la Mamá Grande'. Beyond that, what is most interesting from a historical and political point of view is the notion of the birth of a new era, which remains tantalisingly unexplained, in spite of its aura of promise and intent. Overlooked by many of the story's commentators, the notion would seem to relate closely to two aspects of the narrator's final statement: these are i) the exemplarity of the story that he has now finished telling (a story that he anticipates will be 'lección y escarmiento de las generaciones futuras', pp.234–35), and ii) the urgency with which 'la noticia de la Mamá Grande' needs to be broadcast, ahead of the arrival of the municipal street cleaners who will sweep up 'la basura de sus funerales' once and for all, 'por todos los siglos de los siglos' (p.235). Notwithstanding the parodic ring of the claim to exemplarity, redolent of the ironic tone of Cervantes's prologue to his collection of 'Novelas ejemplares' (1613), the reader senses that s/he should, at least in part, take the narrator's discourse at face value. Similarly, the mixture of hyperbole and apocalyptic prospect in the narrator's closing words should not be read as contrary to, or cancelling out, the historiographic mission announced at the very beginning of the story; rather, his words highlight the ideological and generic complexity of 'Los funerales de la Mamá Grande', to which further and more nuanced consideration can now be given.

vii. Modes of fiction

In the light of the foregoing analysis, 'Los funerales de la Mamá Grande' stands out as an impressive amalgam of different narrative styles and representations of the real. The narrator's claim near the end of the story that he is producing a 'chronicle' (p.232) is confirmed to a certain degree in the linear reconstruction of events that start with Mamá Grande's death and continue all the way down to her funeral. However, the vagueness of many temporal markers ('muchos días', 'semanas interminables', etc.) undermines any sense we might have that we are reading a realistic narrative of the kind exemplified elsewhere in the volume. What is more, the frame that surrounds the self-proclaimed chronicle also accommodates the systematic rearrangement of past events and the creation of ironic effects. The term 'crónicas', in the plural, is also used, just once (p.233), to signify complete, encyclopaedic coverage or enumeration of facets of the real world, and the story is full of such enumerations. However, both the claim and the ploy are noticeably self-conscious and playful, and the reader does not believe the narrator's pretence of mimesis any more than s/he believes that the Pope sails in a gondola from Rome to Macondo, in just one night. And yet, we have acknowledged the overall fit between the fictional story of two hundred years of hegemony in Macondo and the conventionally recorded histories of colonial and post-colonial experience in countries such as Colombia and (say) Venezuela, down to the middle of the twentieth century. From this point of view, the narrator's reference to 'la incertidumbre política de los últimos tiempos' (p.221) leading up to Mamá Grande's death demands to be read, at one level, as a notation for the intrusion of savage violence into Colombian politics from 1948 on, in keeping with the historical settings depicted in 'Un día de éstos' and 'La viuda de Montiel'. So, hyperbole and fantasy notwithstanding, we can legitimately read 'Los funerales de la Mamá Grande' as a 'verídica historia' (p. 216), in the terms of a broad allegorical representation of past and contemporary historical experience.

In a detailed reading of 'Los funerales de la Mamá Grande', Judith A. Goetzinger notes a 'transition from the realistic first section [of the story] to [a] fantastic second part' (*40*, p.242) and asserts that it is the business of the narrator to create a folk legend, transforming the events of Mamá Grande's life and death into a myth. While the first of these observations accords generally with the analysis conducted here, the second observation is questionable and requires a broadening of the parameters of the debate so as to take in consideration of the relation between realism and a broad set of terms including fantasy, legend and myth, which can be subsumed under the catch-all label of 'magical realism'. For George McMurray, 'Los funerales de la Mamá Grande' represents an inaugural moment in García Márquez's trajectory, introducing 'a new brand of realism, a realism expanded and enhanced by magical improbabilities and a keen sense of the grotesque and the absurd' (*20*, p.65). This statement captures a good deal of the complexity and flavour of García Márquez's story; we note, however, that such a claim already makes allowance for the presence of a range of elements that exceed the limits of a simple definition. In fact, 'Los funerales de la Mamá Grande' resists attempts at totalizing description, because of the sheer variety of its narrative styles. This has been recognised by David W. Foster in his identification of two contradictory *narrataires* in the story (*38*), and especially by James Higgins who concludes that, 'The story, in effect, has the character of popular oral narrative, privileging the legendary and depicting the world in larger-than-life terms, but at the same time its "magical realism" is counterbalanced by an ironic, irreverent tone which subverts the very legend it is propagating' (*43*, p.144). Higgins' lucid assessment emphasizes that the narrative purpose of 'Los funerales de la Mamá Grande' is at least dual, if not multiple; after all, we should not dismiss the likelihood that, at the same time as it was driven by an imperative to address serious themes of politics and history, the story is also motivated, to a large part, by the desire to entertain.

In spite of these complexities and qualifications, a broadly-defined 'magical realism' remains a useful critical tool for understanding and classifying 'Los funerales de la Mamá Grande'. The story approximates closely to the type of magical-realist narrative proposed by Stephen Slemon as long ago as 1986. In what has proved to be an influential essay, Slemon focussed on magical-realist narratives within a post-colonial context and postulated three key features, including 'the foreshortening of history so that the time scheme of the [story] metaphorically contains the long process of colonization and its aftermath'. As argued above, 'Los funerales de la Mamá Grande' offers an allegorical depiction of colonial and post-colonial social relations in a tropical Hispanic environment, which mirrors exactly that stratagem of representation. García Márquez's story also exemplifies the 'transformational realism' referred to by Slemon, where 'the site of the [magical-realist] text, though described in familiar and local terms, is metonymic of the postcolonial culture as a whole' (*80*, p.411). There is also a close, if not absolute, correspondence between 'Los funerales de la Mamá Grande' and Slemon's third criterion or property of magical-realist narrative. That criterion is formulated as 'the thematic foregrounding of those gaps, absences, and silences produced by the colonial encounter and reflected in the text's disjunctive language of narration'. 'On this third level,' Slemon adds, 'the magic-realist texts tend to display a preoccupation with images of borders and [centres] and to work toward destabilizing their fixity' (*80*, pp.411–12). It is certainly true that 'Los funerales de la Mamá Grande' asserts thematically the positive value of the margin against the spurious authority of the centre; also, that the narrator's discourse presents itself as a deliberate challenge to 'el blablablá histórico' of officialdom (p.229). However, the gulf between his discourse and the pervasive ignorance and self-deception of the common people is of a different order from Slemon's 'disjunctive language of narration', which is better illustrated, perhaps, in the conflicting perspectives of *Cien años de soledad*. There, García Márquez will

articulate a conflict between two versions or visions of history and
self-determination, around various members of the Buendía family
(from Ursula to the last Aureliano) and other, less mystified citizens
of Macondo, who respond to the impositions of colonialism and
neo-colonialism in quite different, and salutary ways. As interpreted
by a long line of critics stretching down to Alfred J. López (*70*), the
differences in outlook between the Buendías and the non-Buendías
work well as an illustration of Slemon's 'metaphysical clash or
double vision inherent in colonial history and language' (*80*, p.420):
in fact, I suspect that Slemon derived his three-pronged model of the
magical realist narrative precisely from García Márquez's practice
in *Cien años de soledad*.

The engagement of 'Los funerales de la Mamá Grande' with
post-colonial circumstance is nonetheless significant and endows
the text with powerful contemporary relevance centring on the
themes of political instability and the birth of a new era. The notion
of the birth of a new era responds, I believe, to a dual motivation.
First and foremost, it is a logical consequence of events within the
world of the text where the death of Mamá Grande — long overdue
— is more than likely to result in the collapse of the anachronistic
system of which she is the bloated and corrupt embodiment. In
addition to this, we can assume an extra-textual stimulus for change
in the community's attitude. If we extrapolate from the fictional
realm of Macondo to contemporary circumstance in northern
Colombia and, more generally, throughout the Caribbean basin,
then we encounter a regional context of 'incertidumbre política'
(p.221) whose most dramatic manifestation, and the one with the
widest reverberations, has to be the Cuban Revolution, begun
inauspiciously in December 1956 and rounded off with the
triumphant entry of Fidel Castro's guerrilla troops into La Habana,
from which the dictator Fulgencio Batista had already fled, in
January 1959.[3] Political history and allegorical narrative are
brought crucially into alignment in this reading. The death of

---

[3] On the Cuban Revolution, the standard narrative account continues to be
that of Hugh Thomas, *Cuba or the Pursuit of Freedom* (London: Eyre &
Spottiswoode, 1971).

feudal, colonial and neo-colonial practices in the fictional realm of Macondo coincides with the birth of a new moral and political order on the Caribbean island that will promptly become the focus of the world's attention and various expectations. It is here that the date of composition and moment of enunciation of García Márquez's narrative acquire their fullest import. Written in May and June 1959, 'Los funerales de la Mamá Grande' captures and translates the seismic shift affecting the political order of the hispanophone and non-hispanophone Caribbean, and that of the world beyond. Poised at the moment of schism, it is no surprise that the narrative should be inspired by a sense of urgency about registering the details of a national and international commotion before historians of a different persuasion turn up and appropriate events for their own agendas. If this extended allegorical reading is valid, then 'Los funerales de la Mamá Grande' may be seen as occupying a prominent place within the cultural and discursive space surrounding the historical processes of decolonisation and, eventually, the tricontinentalism that will radiate out from Cuba in the mid- 1960s.[4] Through the vehicles of magical realism and post-colonial allegory,[5] 'Los funerales de la Mamá Grande' bears witness to the birth of a new order, initiating at the same time a new style and period in the author's literary career.

---

[4] For an authoritative analysis of 'tricontinentalism' and the Caribbean, see Robert J. C. Young, *Postcolonialism: an Historical Introduction* (Oxford: Blackwell, 2001), especially pp. 4–6 and 204–16.

[5] I sound a deliberate and partial echo, here, of Fredric Jameson's once celebrated work on 'Third World Allegory', not so much for its possible relevance to 'Los funerales de la Mamá Grande' as for the link, clearly consonant with my interpretation of García Márquez's story, that Jameson establishes between satire and the utopian impulse: 'All satire', Jameson observes, 'necessarily carries a utopian frame of reference within itself.' See 'Third-world Literature in the Era of Multinational Capitalism', in Michael Hardt & Kathi Weeks, eds., *The Jameson Reader* (Oxford: Blackwell, 2000), pp. 315–39 (p. 330).

viii. Relations with later work, and differentiation from a source text

There is no doubt that 'Los funerales de la Mamá Grande' occupies a pivotal position in García Márquez's output, anticipating the style and conceptual design of later works including the novels, *Cien años de soledad* (1967) and *El otoño del patriarca* (1975), and most of the stories in *La increíble y triste historia de la cándida Eréndira y su abuela desalmada* (1972). The ultimate fate of the *criollo* order in *Cien años de soledad* will re-play, on a grand apocalyptic scale, the death of Mamá Grande and the regime that she embodied, whilst in the 1975 novel her unnatural longevity and stranglehold over the people's imagination will crystallise again in the figures of the patriarch and his mother, Bendición Alvarado. In the wider context of Colombian fiction of the mid- twentieth century, 'Los funerales de la Mamá Grande' also stands in an enlightening relationship to a slightly earlier text written by one of García Márquez's compatriots, Jorge Zalamea (Bogotá 1905–70). As first noted by Mario Vargas Llosa (*28*, pp.166–69), *El gran Burundún-Burundá ha muerto* (1952) and the companion story, 'La metamorfosis de su Excelencia' (1949), provide a template for García Marquez's narrative of the death-throes and burial of a potentate. The backbone of Zalamea's novella is a massively-attended 'marcha triunfal y fúnebre' (*82,* p. 9) which culminates in a massacre of civilians gunned down by troops loyal to the great Dictator. The momentary focus on the Dictator's 'ataúd de plomo' (*82*, p. 24) and the invocation of his name as 'el eco de un largo eructo' (*82*, p.13) are details which García Márquez will reproduce at key moments in the story of Mamá Grande's death and burial, along with a highly rhetorical style including lists and exaggeration. The boastful insistence on 'la verdad histórica' (*82*, p.11) of a 'crónica veraz' (*82*, p.50) foreshadows identical claims made in 'Los funerales de la Mamá Grande', mixed in with ingredients of grotesque humour and political satire that are also common to both works. In view of this amount of detailed overlap, the reader could be forgiven for regarding 'Los funerales de la Mamá Grande' as a rather slavish re-make of *El gran Burundún-Burundá ha muerto*.

However, to adopt that view would be to overlook crucial differences between the two texts, in which the specificity of García Márquez's story resides. A major difference is the lengthened historical perspective of the narrative of 'Los funerales de la Mamá Grande', which stretches far back into the colonial period of Spanish American history and invests the story with an allegorical dimension not developed in Zalamea's novella. Second, the presence of a frame around the raw material of Mamá Grande's life and death creates perspectives of irony and critique which the reader of 'Los funerales de la Mamá Grande' can occupy alongside a narrator who possesses superior insight into the workings of the fictional world he presents. Most important of all, perhaps, is the formal stratagem adopted by García Márquez of guiding his narrative towards the brink of momentous change. Through this device 'Los funerales de la Mamá Grande' acquires pointed political significance in relation to current events in Cuba (see above) and, within the wider context of the Caribbean, to the situation in Venezuela after General Marcos Pérez Jiménez's fall from power in January 1958.[6] Coincidence with a historical watershed brings out the full political potential of Zalamea's novella, which had failed to provide a precise frame of reference for the scenario of tyranny and repression sketched out in its pages. A comparative perspective that registers this and other differences confirms the added value of García Márquez's adaptation of *El gran Burundún-Burundá ha muerto* and underscores the profound topicality of 'Los funerales de la Mamá Grande'.

---

[6] Complementary accounts of García Márquez in Caracas at the time of the fall of Pérez Jiménez can be consulted in Plinio Apuleyo Mendoza (*73,* pp.33–41) and Stephen Minta (*74,* pp.57–58).

Conclusion

In this Critical Guide I have sought to account in a variety of ways for the eight stories that make up the collection, *Los funerales de la Mamá Grande*. First and foremost, I have looked closely at the stories in terms of their individual formal characteristics and various interrelationships; beyond that, I have paid attention to connections with earlier and later works by García Márquez and with works by fellow Colombian and Spanish American writers such as Jorge Zalamea and Jorge Luis Borges; finally, I have located the stories against a broad comparative backdrop featuring non-Hispanic authors such as Euripides, Kafka, Faulkner, Chekhov, and Hemingway. In this way, I hope to have conveyed a sense of the author's multiple objectives and achievements in each and all of the stories in the volume.

Regarding the established critical tradition, I have chosen quite deliberately to break with precedent by adopting a chronological approach to the stories. Whilst this strategy has been somewhat out of synch with the order in which the stories have appeared in all published editions, it has made it possible for me to trace certain patterns of evolution and variation in the collection, especially as regards mode and the narratorial stance on the moral and political issues addressed in the stories. In respect of mode, we have witnessed a process of evolution and transformation in García Márquez's writing between 1947 and 1959, moving from an initial engagement with Kafka, through Faulkner and Hemingway, to the mimicking of popular oral narrative in the title story of *FMG*. In relation to the other items in the volume, 'Los funerales de la Mamá Grande' stands out most conspicuously through its abandonment of the Hemingway-esque and Chekhovian realism of 'La siesta del martes' and 'Las rosas artificiales', for example, also superseding the Faulknerian aesthetic of 'Un día después del sábado' and other

earlier writings. At the same time, the title story's roots lie quite clearly in the author's 1952 essays on La Sierpe, which consequently emerge as a crucial point of reference in García Márquez's creative process before his accession to fame with *Cien años de soledad.*

Viewed retrospectively, 'Los funerales de la Mamá Grande' confers a perceptible unity on the collection which it brings to a close. Most noticeably, it enlarges the picture of death and corruption drawn with clinical precision in 'La viuda de Montiel' and embodied in the symbolic motifs of corpses (cf. the ending of 'La prodigiosa tarde de Baltazar'), decayed teeth ('Un día de éstos'), dead birds ('Un día después del sábado'), and wilted flowers ('La siesta del martes'). The suggestion of a new start heralded near the end of 'Los funerales de la Mamá Grande' projects a shaft of light in retrospect onto the counter-types and symbols of courage, determination and generosity of spirit that stood out against a background of prevailing institutional indifference and negativity in the earlier stories.

From the vantage point that it establishes over the collection as a whole, 'Los funerales de la Mamá Grande' brings into focus a number of thematic syntheses, including fractured families and the recurrent motif of enigma. The theme of the family is Oedipally-inflected in 'Un día después del sábado' and 'En este pueblo no hay ladrones', and tinged with sadness in 'La siesta del martes' and 'Rosas artificiales'. Enigma takes the form of a literal puzzle ('acertijo') in 'Un día después del sábado', where the figure of the old man credited with inventing the crossword in a provincial backwater may be a homage to Jorge Luis Borges; other enigmas include the 'black holes' in the narrative architecture of 'Rosas artificiales' and the understated intimation of epochal change near the end of 'Los funerales de la Mamá Grande'. Also running like a thread through the collection are problems with knowledge and perception. First articulated around the characters of the priest and the young man from Manaure in 'El día después del sábado', they reappear later in 'Rosas artificiales' where a witless mother is kept on the side-lines of a drama affecting her daughter, who is almost certainly pregnant. In the two final stories, partial knowledge is inseparable from ideology and the false consciousness of individuals who might otherwise be independent-minded and free.

An area of critical debate in which I have sought to intervene is that of García Márquez's sensitivity to issues of gender. There is a strand of opinion in the criticism devoted to his work that regards him as complicit with machismo and a purveyor of gender-stereotypes (see *62*). In several chapters of this Guide, I take issue with these assumptions and offer what I regard as a more accurate reading of García Márquez's stance on gender. In the chapter on 'En este pueblo no hay ladrones', I make use of formal analysis to reveal a dialectic between a masculinist and a woman-centered perspective on the substantive issues dealt with in the story. The subsequent pairing of 'Rosas artificiales' and 'La viuda de Montiel' emphasizes the prominence, in García Márquez's work and outlook, of the difficulties and concerns faced by women under patriarchy — a major point of convergence with Anton Chekhov. Sensitivity to women's experiences and needs is turned inside out in 'Los funerales de la Mamá Grande', where the narrative dramatises attitudes of extreme misogyny and contempt; the roots of the legend of 'la marquesita de la Sierpe' in northern Colombian folklore set the story of Mamá Grande apart from the contemporary intellectual climate that gave rise to studies such as Erich Neumann's analysis of the archetype of 'The Great Mother'.

In addition to focussing on the textual and cultural specificities of the stories in *FMG*, a key objective of the present Guide has been to highlight García Márquez's mastery of, and contribution to the short story form. To this end, I have conducted a systematic analysis of each of the stories' narrative and poetic features, which combine in an impressive variety of configurations. I have also drawn comparisons with texts by a range of writers who are acknowledged masters of the *cuento* form: Chekhov, Borges and Hemingway, amongst others. This exercise gives a fascinating insight into the possibilities of comparative literature based around the stories of García Márquez. Always acknowledging their rooted-ness in a Latin American context, comparative literary study can do as much as any other methodology to expose the workings and explain the profound appeal of a volume of stories that speak to successive generations of readers — male and female, hispanophone and non-Spanish speaking, and of different ages — on a range of subjects including history and politics, morality and art, desire and imagination, love and sex: in short, many of the fundamentals of the human condition and their manifestation in and through culture.

Bibliography

A. GARCÍA MÁRQUEZ'S AUTOBIOGRAPHICAL MEMOIRS

1. *Vivir para contarla* (Barcelona: Mondadori, 2002). Offers a mine of information about the political and life-circumstances surrounding the composition of the stories and key moments in the author's career; the narrative stops at 1955.

B. BIOGRAPHY OF GARCÍA MÁRQUEZ

2. Saldívar, Dasso, *García Márquez. El viaje a la semilla. La biografía* (Madrid: Alfaguara, 1997). The definitive study to date, rich in contextual data pertaining to the author's life before and after the Cuban Revolution, and equipped with a useful bibliography.

C. INTERVIEWS WITH GARCÍA MÁRQUEZ

3. Fernández-Braso, Miguel, *Gabriel García Márquez (una conversación infinita)* (Madrid: Azur, 1969). In spite of its slimness, this comparatively early volume provides worthwhile coverage of topics ranging from literary influences and political views to language and the fictional representation of women.
4. Mendoza, Plinio Apuleyo, *Gabriel García Márquez. El olor de la guayaba. Conversaciones con Plinio Apuleyo Mendoza* (Barcelona: Bruguera, 1982). Records conversations ranging across the author's life, his sense of cultural identity, favoured literary models, and many other topics.

D. COLLECTED JOURNALISM AND OTHER PRIMARY SOURCE MATERIAL

5. Gabriel García Márquez, *Obra periodística*, 4 vols., ed. Jacques Gilard (Barcelona: Bruguera, 1981–83). Compilation of the author's

journalism on matters ranging from current affairs and travel to film criticism and literature.

6. *La soledad de América latina: Brindis por la poesía* (Cali: Corporación de Editorial Universitaria de Colombia, 1983). Contains the author's Nobel Prize address of 1983, an English translation of which appears under the title 'The Solitude of Latin America' in *19*, pp. 207–11.

E. BOOKS THAT CONTAIN DISCUSSION OF THE STORIES, AND OTHER RELEVANT MATERIAL

7. Alfaro, Gustavo, *Constante de la historia de Latinoamérica en García Márquez* (Cali, Colombia: Biblioteca Banco Popular, 1979), 61–70. Generally unsophisticated readings of the stories in *FMG*; accounts for the title story as an 'epopeya satírica del caciquismo' (p. 61).
8. Bell-Villada, Gene H., *García Márquez: the Man and his Work* (Chapel Hill: University of North Carolina Press, 1990). Pays serious attention to the stories, seeing them as among the author's greatest achievements; more perceptive on the shortest stories (eg. 'Rosas artificiales') than the longest, which Bell-Villada dismisses provocatively as the weakest in the collection.
9. Benedetti, Mario, Emmanuel Carballo, et al (eds.), *9 Asedios a García Márquez* (Santiago de Chile: Editorial Universitaria, 1969). Contains pioneering studies by Rama (*52*), Vargas Llosa and Volkenning (*56*) that are remarkable for their commitment, intelligence and timing, even if they have since been superseded.
10. Bloom, Harold (ed.), *Modern Critical Views. Gabriel García Márquez* (New York: Chelsea House Publishers, 1989). A major anthology of essays on the Márquez opus, including *48* and *51* below.
11. Carrillo, Germán D., *La narrativa de Gabriel García Márquez* (Madrid: Ediciones de Arte y Bibliofilia, 1975), pp.111–23. The pages devoted to *FMG* provide succinct sketches of the plots and thematic outlines of each of the stories.
12. Collazos, Oscar, *García Márquez: la soledad y la gloria. Su vida y su obra* (Barcelona: Plaza y Janés, 1983), pp.74–89. The section on *FMG* comprises terse appreciations of each of the stories, which are in fact more varied in tone than Collazos allows. Confirms the impact on García Márquez of events surrounding the fall of General Pérez Jiménez in Caracas, Venezuela in January 1958 (pp.60–62).
13. Earle, Peter G. (ed.), *Gabriel García Márquez* (Madrid: Taurus, 1981). Belonging to the 'El escritor y la crítica' series, this volume collates much valuable material about the writer and his works, including item *46* below.

14. Foster, David W., *Studies in the Spanish American Short Story* (Columbia & London: University of Missouri Press, 1979). Contains sophisticated analyses of two of the stories in *FMG* (see *37* and *38*).

15. González Echevarría, Roberto, *The Voice of the Masters. Writing and Authority in Modern Latin American Literature* (Austin: University of Texas Press, 1985), pp.56–60. Considers the title story as 'a sort of sequel to or meta-end of *Doña Bárbara*', the earlier classic novel of the land by Venezuelan Rómulo Gallegos (p.57).

16. Hernández de López, Ana María (ed.), *En el punto de mira: Gabriel García Márquez* (Madrid: Pliegos, 1985). Contains three essays on stories in *FMG*: *31*, *44* & *49*.

17. Herrera Molina, Luis Carlos, S.J., *El cuento, estructura y símbolo. Análisis tentativo de los cuentos de Gabriel García Márquez* (Bogotá: Pontificia Universidad Javeriana, 1998). Analyses each of the stories in *FMG* and puts forwards interpretations that differ markedly from those offered in this Guide, especially as regards the connotations of the priest-figures in the collection.

18. Janes, Regina, *Gabriel García Márquez. Revolutions in Wonderland* (Columbia: University of Missouri Press, 1981), pp.35–44. Makes genuinely interesting observations about all of the stories, which are treated as an organic and evolving whole. Especially good on 'Los funerales de la Mamá Grande', which is seen as politicizing the 'folkloric impossibilities of La Sierpe' (p.44).

19. McGuirk, Bernard, & Richard Cardwell, *Gabriel García Márquez: New Readings* (Cambridge: Cambridge University Press, 1987). Contains two indispensable essays on the stories (*34* & *41*) and an English translation of García Márquez's 1982 Nobel Prize acceptance address, 'The Solitude of Latin America' (pp. 207–11).

20. McMurray, George R., *Gabriel García Márquez* (New York: Frederick Ungar, 1977), pp.47–66. Long on plot-summary but has worthwhile things to say about 'La viuda de Montiel' and the title-story. Draws attention to links with Hemingway and remarks pertinently on García Márquez's 'traditional Chekhovian approach to the genre' in terms of delineation of character or situations 'viewed from the perspective of the neutral, omniscient narrator' (p.47).

21. — (ed.), *Critical Essays on Gabriel García Márquez* (Boston, Mass: G.K. Hall & Co., 1987). Headed by an authoritative introduction, this volume reproduces some early reviews and important essays by Foster (*38*) and Oberhelman (*48*), amongst others.

22. Oberhelman, Harley, *Gabriel García Márquez. A Study of the Short Fiction* (Boston: Twayne, 1991), pp.19–35. The pages on *FMG* provide useful syntheses of critical opinion on each of the stories.

Good on name-symbolism and Baltazar's 'Christ-like image' (p. 27) in 'La prodigiosa tarde de Baltazar'.

23. — *The Presence of Hemingway in the Short Fiction of Gabriel García Márquez* (Fredericton, Canada: York Press Ltd, 1994). Slim but meaty volume documenting connections between the work of the two writers.

24. Pelayo, Rubén, *Gabriel García Márquez: a Critical Companion* (Westport, CT: Greenwood Press, 2001). Pedagogically oriented, with fragmented commentary on aspects of 'La siesta del martes', 'La prodigiosa tarde de Baltazar' and 'Los funerales de la Mamá Grande'.

25. Pupo-Walker, Enrique (ed.), *El cuento hispanoamericano ante la crítica* (Madrid: Castalia, 1973). Contains a useful introduction surveying the history of the form in Spanish America, and a clutch of essays on a wide range of authors including García Márquez. See *50* below.

26. — (co-ord.), *El cuento hispanoamericano* (Madrid: Castalia, 1995). In a similar format to *25*, but with two essays on García Márquez: one, an in-depth study of 'La siesta del martes' (*36*), the other, a selective overview of various stories (*33*).

27. Tittler, Jonathan (ed.), *Violencia y literatura en Colombia* (Madrid: Orígenes, 1989). Includes an important essay on the influence of Hemingway (*41*) and a second on women and violence in *Cien años de soledad* (*71*).

28. Vargas Llosa, Mario, *García Márquez: historia de un deicidio* (Barcelona: Barral & Caracas: Monte Avila, 1971). A pioneering study that is still essential reading more than thirty years after the first edition appeared. Provides a wealth of background information and detailed interpretation of each of the stories, which are seen as staging a conflict between subjective or oneiric perspectives of the real, on the one hand, and the category of 'lo real objetivo', on the other; argues that the latter is displaced by the former as the collection evolves.

29. Waters Hood, Edward, *La ficción de Gabriel García Márquez. Repetición e intertextualidad* (New York: Peter Lang, 1993). A methodical rather than insightful study of intertextuality in works including the stories of *FMG*. Informative on 'La siesta del martes' and 'Un día de éstos'.

30. Williams, Raymond, *Gabriel García Márquez* (Boston, Mass: Twayne, 1984). A leading commentator on García Márquez, Williams situates the collection in what he terms the author's 'middle years', 1956–1962, and relates the stories to other writings of the period including *El coronel no tiene quien le escriba* and *La mala hora*. Surveys all eight stories, starting with the last-written, which gives the study an unusual non-chronological slant. Shares David W. Foster's (*37* & *38*) interest in the fictional construction of a reader, which

informs the comments on 'La prodigiosa tarde de Baltazar' and the title story.

F. STUDIES REFERRING TO ONE OR MORE OF THE STORIES AND/OR THEIR PRECURSORS

31. Arrington, Melvin S. Jr., '"La viuda de Montiel": un retrato en miniatura de Macondo', in *16*, pp.63–70. Slight study which discerns a stylistic mix of irony, fantasy and satire in the named story, which, it is argued, foreshadows the writing style of *Cien años de soledad.*

32. Bell-Villada, Gene H., 'What the Young Gabriel García Márquez Learned from the Master Graham Greene: The Case of "Un día de éstos"', *The Comparatist*, 24 (May 2000), pp.146–56. Unearths a precursor of 'Un día de éstos' in an episode of Greene's *The Power and the Glory.*

33. Burgos, Fernando, 'Aspectos de la cuentística de Gabriel García Márquez', in *26*, pp. 453–72. Summarises the history of the *cuento* in Spanish America and provides useful comments on several stories including, from the early years, 'La tercera resignación' and 'Eva está dentro de su gato'.

34. Cardwell, Richard, 'Characterization in the Early Fiction of Gabriel García Máquez', in *19*, pp.5–16. Perceptive study of characterization in 'Un día de éstos' and 'La siesta del martes'.

35. Dauster, Frank, 'The Short Stories of García Márquez', *Books Abroad*, 47, 3 (1973), pp. 466–70. Superficial commentary on some of the stories, supplying useful fuel for disagreement and debate.

36. Fiddian, Robin W., '"La siesta del martes" de Gabriel García Márquez', in *26*, pp.411–25. Wrongly gives the date of composition of this story, after Peel and others, as 1948; reads the plot in archetypal terms, also drawing connections with Euripides, as in the present Guide.

37. Foster, David W., 'García Márquez and the *Ecriture* of Complicity: "La prodigiosa tarde de Baltazar"', in *14*, pp.39–50. On the textual engagement of the reader, who is meant to enter into a relation of complicity with the narrative presentation of the character, Baltazar.

38. — 'The Double Inscription of the *Narrataire* in "Los funerales de la Mamá Grande', in *14*, pp. 51–62; also in *21*, pp.102–113. A narratological approach to the title-story which envisages two 'receptors' of the narrative: the first is complicit with the story's myth-mongering whilst the second conducts a reading that is critical and 'demythifying'.

39. Gilard, Jacques, 'Prólogos' to volumes I, II, and IV of the author's collected journalistic writings cited in *5* above. Highly informative on

links between Márquez's journalism and the political sphere, also on the chronology of his early writings; provides detailed coverage of writings on film and on 'La Sierpe'. An indispensable research tool.

40. Goetzinger, Judith A., 'The Emergence of Folk Myth in "Los funerales de la Mamá Grande', *Revista de Estudios Hispánicos,* 6 (1972), pp.237–48. A relatively early study of the title-story, which it analyses usefully in terms of structure and narrative tone; concludes by relating the story to others in the collection, which share a common vision of decay.

41. González, Eduardo, 'Beware of Gift-bearing Tales: Reading "Baltazar's Prodigious Afternoon" according to Marcel Mauss', in *19*, pp.17–32. Theoretically- informed reading of this story, which I address in Chapter 3 of this Guide.

42. Hayes, Aden W., 'Hemingway y García Márquez: Tarde y temprano', in *27*, pp.53–62. Reproduces several statements by the author acknowledging the importance of Hemingway, amongst them the self-deprecating assessment of 'La mujer que llegaba a las seis' as 'más de Hemingway que de G[abriel] G[arcía] M[árquez]'; detects the American writer's influence on 'La siesta del martes', amongst other stories.

43. Higgins, James, 'Gabriel García Márquez: *Cien años de soledad*', in Philip Swanson (ed.), *Landmarks in Modern Latin American Fiction* (London: Routledge, 1990), pp.141–60 (144). In spite of its brevity, a single paragraph on 'Los funerales de la Mamá Grande' provides one of the most intelligent readings ever of the title-story and throws light on its status as a precursor of *Cien años de soledad.*

44. Kason, Nancy M., 'El arte del ambiente psicológico en "Un día de éstos"', in *16*, pp.83–90. Focuses on the skilful creation of an atmosphere of hostility in this story, where echoes of Hemingway are discerned in the description of the dentist's extraction of the mayor's tooth without anaesthetic.

45. Kilmer-Tchalekian, Mary A., 'Nabo, el negro a quien García Márquez hizo volar', *Journal of Spanish Studies: Twentieth Century*, 6, 1 (Spring 1978), pp.29–37. Finds the clear imprint of Faulkner in an early story.

46. McGrady, Donald, 'Acerca de una colección desconocida de relatos por Gabriel García Márquez', *Thesaurus* (Bogotá), XXVII (1972), pp.293–320; also reproduced in *13,* pp.60–80. Early study of the first uncollected stories, beginning with 'La otra costilla de la muerte' of 1948 and going up to 1954; features relevant comments on 'Nabo, el negro que hizo esperar a los ángeles' and the author's pseudo-anthropological writings on La Sierpe.

47. Meckled, S., 'The Theme of the Double: an Essential Element throughout García Márquez's Works', *The Crane Bag* (Dublin), 6 (1982), pp.108–117. Illuminating psychological approach to fantastic motifs in a number of texts by García Márquez including some of the early stories; also features in-depth discussion of the author's 'Mother Right ideology' (p. 112).

48. Oberhelman, Harley D., 'William Faulkner and Gabriel García Márquez: Two Nobel Laureates', in *21*, pp.67–79. Documents parallels between a range of works by Faulkner and García Márquez and offers brief but helpful comments on the stories in *FMG*.

49. Paiewonsky-Conde, Edgar, 'La escritura como acto revolucionario: "Los funerales de la Mamá Grande"', in *16*, pp.33–53. Perceptive on major aspects of the story and especially good on the narrator's demythifying function. Takes issue with earlier interpretations including those of Vargas Llosa (*28*) and Goetzinger (*40*), and concludes that, in terms of contributing to revolutionary politics, the author's pen is as mighty as the sword.

50. Peel, Roger M., 'Los cuentos de García Márquez', in *25*, pp.235–48. Not all the dates given are accurate, but the essay deals with most of the stories in *FMG* and offers detailed readings.

51. Plummer, William, 'The Faulkner Relation', in *10*, pp.33–47. Circumspect about multiple borrowings from Faulkner in *La hojarasca* and the subsequent abandoning of what, in the final analysis, proved to be an inappropriate model.

52. Rama, Ángel, 'Un novelista de la violencia americana', in *9*, pp.106–25. First penned in 1964, this essay shows a fine appreciation of García Márquez's prose style, which it compares briefly with those of Chekhov and Hemingway. Excellent on the 'a-historic, almost mythical world-view' of the society depicted in 'Un día después del sábado', and generally good on the thematics of violence in works written before *Cien años de soledad*.

53. — 'La iniciación literaria de Gabriel García Márquez', *Texto Crítico*, I, 1 (January 1975), pp.5–13. Perceptive on the early influences operating on García Márquez, whom Rama represents in the early 1950s as being torn between Faulkner and Hemingway; offers insightful discussion of 'realismo de lo irreal' and accounts convincingly for the place of 'La mujer que llegaba a las seis' in the author's development.

54. Rodríguez Monegal, Emir, 'Novedad y anacronismo de *Cien años de soledad*', *Maga* (Panamá), 4 (October–December1984), pp.92–109. Retrospective study identifying several features that will develop and crystallise in the landmark novel of 1967. Perceptive on different treatments of violence in 'Un día de éstos' and *La mala hora*; less persuasive criticism of the title story, but an important point of reference nonetheless.

55. Ruiz R., Hugo, 'Notas sobre la obra de García Márquez', *Boletín Cultural y Bibliográfico* (Bogotá) X, 1 (1967), pp.140–43. Commends his compatriot for accurately depicting 'determinadas situaciones y personajes propios de nuestro ambiente y nuestra historia' (p.142).

56. Volkenning, Ernesto, 'Gabriel García Márquez o el trópico desembrujado', in *9*, pp.147–63. First published in Bogotá in 1963, this essay is a landmark in early criticism of García Márquez's work. Polemically downplays the importance of Faulkner to the Colombian author's literary development, stressing instead the exactness of his representation of the world of the tropics and cult of human individuality. Good on 'La siesta del martes'.

G. BACKGROUND AND OTHER COMPLEMENTARY MATERIAL

57. Andrew, Dudley, *André Bazin* (New York: Oxford University Press, 1978). Authoritative study of the French film-theorist and pedagogue. Pages 113–131 foreground a sympathetic discussion of Bazin's commitment to realism in the cinema (especially Jean Renoir) and his subsequent predilection for Italian neo-realism (especially Rossellini).

58. Bazin, André, *What is Cinema?* Essays selected and translated by Hugh Gray (Berkeley & Los Angeles: University of California Press, 1967). Contains 'The Evolution of the Language of Cinema', pp. 23–40, where Bazin, writing of the films of Rosselini, De Sica et al., claims that they perfected realism and captured reality as a continuum and in all its mystery.

59. Borges, Jorge Luis, 'El arte narrativo y la magia', in *Obras completas*, 3 vols. (Barcelona: Emecé, 1989), I, pp.226–32.

60. Chekhov, Anton, *About Love and Other Stories*, translated with an introduction by Rosamund Bartlett (Oxford: Oxford University Press, 2004).

61. Cortázar, Julio, 'Algunos aspectos del cuento', *Casa de las Américas*, II, 15–16 (1962), pp.3–14; reproduced in the author's three-part *Obra crítica*, 2, ed. Jaime Alazraki (Madrid: Alfaguara, 1994), pp.365–85. A personal view of the short story, coinciding, as it happens, with the year of publication of *FMG*.

62. Damjanova, Ludmila, 'Marvel Moreno y Gabriel García Márquez: escritura femenina y escritura masculina', in *69* below, pp. 258–302. Takes García Márquez to task for alleged gender-stereotyping in his fiction

63. Euripides, *Suppliant Women; Electra; Heracles*, ed. & trans. David Kovacs for the Loeb Classical Library (Cambridge, Mass., & London: Harvard University Press, 1998).

64. Fiddian, Robin W., 'Two Aspects of Technique in *El coronel no tiene quien le escriba*', *Neophilologus*, 69 (1985), pp.386–93. On animal references and Christian imagery in the early novella.

65. — 'From Film to Book: García Márquez and the Neo-realist Aesthetic', *Cine-Lit V. Essays on Hispanic Film and Fiction*, eds. George Cabello-Castellet, Jaume Martí-Olivella & Guy H. Wood (Corvallis, Oregon: Cine-Lit Publications, 2004), pp.7–13. Looks at some of the author's 1950s film reviews and finds close connections with his theory and practice as a writer.

66. García Lorca, Federico, 'La monja gitana', in *Obras completas*, 16th ed. (Madrid: Aguilar, 1971), pp.433–34.

67. Hemingway, Ernest, *The Short Stories of Ernest Hemingway* (New York: Charles Scribner's Sons, 1987).

68. — *Ernest Hemingway on Writing*, ed. Larry W. Phillips (New York: Touchstone, 1999). Important compilation of statements about the art of writing.

69. Jaramillo, María Mercedes, Betty Osorio & Angela Inés Robledo (eds.), *Literatura y cultura. Narrativa colombiana del siglo XX*, 3 vols. (Bogotá: Ministerio de Cultura, 2000). Volume III contains a pertinent essay by Ludmila Damjanova (*62*).

70. López, Alfred J., *Posts and Pasts: a Theory of Postcolonialism* (Albany, NY: State University of New York Press, 2001), pp.150–65. In spite of numerous misprints, solecisms and mistranslations from Spanish, Chapter V of this book contains much interesting material relating García Márquez to Alejo Carpentier and Salman Rushdie.

71. Marcos, Juan Manuel, 'Mujer y violencia en *Cien años de soledad*', in *26*, pp.91–95. Has a certain, oblique relevance to the interpretation of 'En este pueblo no hay ladrones' that is put forward in this Guide.

72. Marting, Diane E., 'The End of Eréndira's Prostitution', *Hispanic Review*, 69 (2001), pp.175–90. Focuses on a famous later story featuring prostitution and insists on García Márquez's 'interest in criticizing aspects of women's oppression' (p.176).

73. Mendoza, Plinio Apuleyo, 'Gabriel García Márquez: el caso perdido', in *La llama y el hielo* (Barcelona: Planeta, 1984), pp.9–150. Less well-known than *4*, this essay is a rich narrative account of the author's friendship with García Márquez beginning in the mid-nineteen fifties. It covers the two men's shared experiences as journalists and *compadres* in Europe 1955–57, Venezuela 1958–59, Cuba 1959–60, and Stockholm in 1983.

74. Minta, Stephen, *Gabriel García Márquez: Writer of Colombia* (London: Jonathan Cape, 1987). Does not comment directly on any of the stories, but sets the author's work firmly in the context of national and regional political history. A useful English-language alternative to Gilard (*39*) and Mendoza (*73*).

75. Neumann, Erich, *The Great Mother: an Analysis of the Archetype*. Trans. from the German by Ralph Mannheim (New York: Bollinger 1955). The classic study of this archetype, ignored in all previous work on the collection in spite of occupying the same time-frame as the essays on La Sierpe.

76. Norwood, Robin, *Women Who Love Too Much* (New York: Simon & Schuster, 1985, and countless reprints). International bestseller about women trapped in dysfunctional heterosexual relationships. Cites case studies that are relevant to women throughout the Western world.

77. Pachón Padilla, Eduardo, *El cuento colombiano*, 4 vols. (Barcelona: Plaza y Janés, 1980–1985). Volume II, 'Generaciones 1955/70', surveys the field surrounding García Márquez.

78. Poggioli, Renato, 'Storytelling in a Double Key', in *The Phoenix and the Spider* (Boston, Mass.: Harvard University Press, 1957), pp.109–130. Insightful study of Chekhov's spirit and narrative artistry.

79. Quiroga, Horacio, 'El manual del perfecto cuentista' (1925), in *Horacio Quiroga. Todos los cuentos*, eds. Napoleón Baccino Ponce de León & Jorge Lafforgue, Colección Archivos (Nanterre: Université Paris X, Centre de Recherches Latino-Americaines; Madrid: Fondo de Cultura Económica, 1993), pp.1189–1191. The same volume also contains 'Los trucos del perfecto cuentista', pp.1191–1193, 'Decálogo del perfecto cuentista', pp. 1194–1195, and 'La retórica del cuento', pp. 1195–1196. Historically important set of theoretical statements concerning the short story.

80. Slemon, Stephen, 'Magical Realism as Postcolonial Discourse', in *Magical Realism: Theory, History, Community*, eds. Lois Parkinson Zamora & Wendy Faris (Durham, NC & London: Duke University Press, 1995), pp.407–26. Seminal reading of *Cien años de soledad* as paradigmatic example of postcolonial discourse, used here to explicate the title story of *FMG*.

81. Woolf, Virginia, 'The Russian Background', in *The Essays of Virginia Woolf*, ed. Andrew McNeillie, 4 vols. Vol. III: 1919–1924 (London: The Hogarth Press, 1988), pp.83–86. Acute comments on Chekhov, later expanded in 'The Russian Point of View' and included in *The Common Reader*, first collection (1925).

82. Zalamea, Jorge, *El Gran Burundún-Burundá ha muerto* (Buenos Aires: Centro Editor de América Latina, 1973). The volume, which is slight, also includes 'Metamorfosis de su Excelencia'.

CRITICAL GUIDES TO SPANISH TEXTS

Edited by
Alan Deyermond and Stephen Hart

CRITICAL GUIDES TO SPANISH TEXTS

Edited by
Alan Deyermond and Stephen Hart